ighly Recommended

Updated as per NCF

OSWAAL BOOKS®

LEARNING MADE SIMPLE

NCERT POORVI NEW TEXTBOOK

NCERT & CBSE

ONE FOR ALL WORKBOOK

CLASS 7

ENGLISH (POORVI)

Workbook with Removable Sheets

10th EDITION

ISBN "9789367477861"

SYLLABUS COVERED

CENTRAL BOARD OF SECONDARY EDUCATION DELHI

Head Office
Oswaal House
1/11, Sahitya Kunj, M.G. Road
Agra-282002 (U.P.), India

R&D Office
1010, Cambourne Business Centre
Cambridge, Cambridgeshire
CB 236DP, United Kingdom

+91-562-2857671

contact@oswaalbooks.com

Curated by

Oswaal Editorial Board

PUBLISHED BY

OSWAAL BOOKS & LEARNING PVT. LTD.

Printed at Alankar Graphics, G.Noida

Contents

All Worksheets solutions can be downloaded from www.oswaalbooks.com or by scanning the QR code here!

Abbreviations:

Questions categorized by CBSE typology: R *Remembering,* U *Understanding,* Ap *Applying,* A *Analysing,* E *Evaluating,* C *Creating.*

CFPQ *(Competency Focused Practice Questions),* A I *Academic Intelligence,* **OEB** *(Oswaal Editorial Board)*

Preface

Uncover#PerfectionThroughPractice with One for All Workbook

Welcome to the One for All Workbook, a comprehensive resource meticulously crafted to guide young minds towards excellence in their academic journey. This workbook is designed as per NCF 2023 to serve as an invaluable companion for students preparing for their Exam.

In today's dynamic educational landscape, where success is synonymous with rigorous practice and a deep understanding of the curriculum, our workbook emerges as a beacon of support for students in **Classes 6th to 9th.** With subjects spanning Mathematics, Science, Social Science, English & Hindi, Sanskrit this workbook is tailored to provide a holistic approach to learning.

What makes CBSE Workbook Classes 6-9 Truly Exceptional?

- **CBSE & NCERT Questions** to recall the concepts for a thorough understanding of the material
- **MCQs,VSA,SA & LA** for diverse & real learning to ensure comprehensive learning.
- **Competency-based Questions** as per NEP to test application of knowledge for a holistic, skill-based approach.
- **Removable Worksheets** to write answers perfectly for extensive practice

May this workbook be your guide and ally as you embark on the path of learning, practice, and growth. Together, let's #PerfectionThroughPractice.

A big shoutout to the super-smart Oswaal Editorial Board, teachers, and subject matter experts for working hard day and night to make this resource awesome. And a sincere thank you to you and all our fellow students for making this tool special.

Your Pals at Team Oswaal Books

Positive Affirmations

An affirmation is a positive statement or phrase that individuals repeat to themselves with the intention of fostering a positive mindset, self-confidence, or personal development. The practice involves affirming desired beliefs or qualities, often in the present tense, to reinforce a positive self-image and encourage a more optimistic outlook.

" EMBRACE YOUR UNIQUENESS, NOURISH SELF-CARE, AND PRESS FORWARD RELENTLESSLY. TO ACHIEVE FLIGHT, UNLOAD THE BAGGAGE THAT SLOWS YOUR ASCENT."

I strongly trust in my vision and work diligently towards making it a reality.

I am capable of learning and growing everyday.

I am not defined by grades & test scores. My true worth lies in my character, compassion and positive impact I have on others.

I celebrate my quirks, for they make me beautifully unique.

I embrace my mistakes, learn from them and use them to fuel my growth & resilience.

My voice matters and I believe in the power of my words to shape the world around me.

I am not the product of circumstances, I am the product of my own choices.

I face challenges with courage and determination.

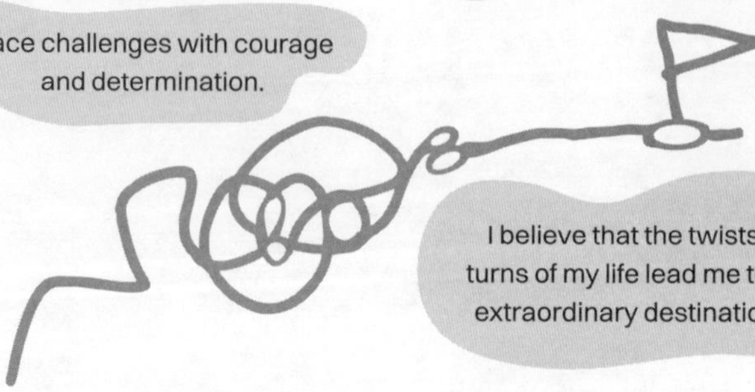

I celebrate the achievements of others without diminishing my journey.

I believe that the twists & turns of my life lead me to an extraordinary destinations.

Exclusive School Books Suppliers

	KARNATAKA
BANGALORE	Pride Book World, 9448685507, Tanwer Books and Garments, 9916049273, Jipsy, 9620325985
MYSORE	Ragavendra Book Agency, 9591911489
	TELANGANA
HYDERABAD	Shri Sharada store Books & Stationers, 9700768789, Sri Balaji Book Depot, 9676996199, Vishal Book Distributors, 9246333166, Pranavi Publishers, 919948853126, Shri Sharada store Books & Stationers, 9700768789
	TAMIL NADU
CHENNAI	M.K. Stores, 9840030099, Sivaa Book Centre, 9952933315, Kamal Book House, 9841077369
ERODE	Selvam Book Centre, 919843199697
MADURAI	Selvi Book Shoppe, 9345037977, Madurai Book Shop, 9751937519
COIMBATORE	CBSC Book Shop, 9585979752
CUDDALORE	Indian Book Centre, 9443093053
	MAHARASHTRA
PUNE	Madhusheela Books & Stationers, 7875899892, Pravin Sales, 8888038889
NANDED	Vijay Book Centre, 9822994436
JALNA	Anil Paper Mart, 919422722522
AURANGABAD	Shree Sainath Agencies, 917350294089, Aarti Book Centre, 919422203836
NAGPUR	Sandeep Book Depot, 9371078789
VASAI	Dinvin Books Excellence PVT. LTD. , 9867561128
MUMBAI	New Student Agencies LLP, 8355965098, Ravechi Book Stationery, 9769002371
	ANDHRA PRADESH
VISAKHAPATNAM	VKML Books, 8125168946, Gupta Brothers Books, 0891- 2754454
NANDYAL	Sathyam Book Store & Fancy, 9052439300
NELLORE	S V S Book Centre, 9347100774
VIJAYAWADA	VKML Books, 9966639957
	HARYANA
ROHTAK	Babu Ram Pradeep Kumar, 9813214692
VIZIANAGARAM	Himamsu Book Distributor, 9493434777
	MADHYA PRADESH
INDORE	Mahesh Book Depot, 9893855543
SHAHDOL	Anjali Book Centre, 917067572992

	JHARKHAND
DEOGHAR	Navyug Sahitya Mandir, 919031917035
BOKARO STEEL CITY	Bokaro Student Friends Pvt. Ltd, 919234628152
	MEGHALAYA
SHILLONG	New Book Centre, 9774088719
	WEST BENGAL
KOLKATA	Oriental Pub. Dist. Pvt. Ltd., 919903879153, United Book House, 9831344622
	UTTAR PRADESH
PRAYAGRAJ	Saraswati book depot, 7706855403
KANPUR(Platinum)	Raj Book, 9235616506
MATHURA	Sapra Traders, 9410076716, Agrawal Book House, 7906527213
GHAZIABAD	Vani Enterprises, 919891276834
	DELHI
DELHI	Mittal Books, 919810133323, Prakash Brothers, 919811179840, R.D. Chawla & Sons, 9810045752, Ameen Global Services, 919716028892, Need Prakashan Pvt Ltd, 9968383261
	GUJARAT
VADODARA	Career Skills Education and Research Foundation, 8469149288
BHARUCH	J.D.Agency, 9099944480
	KERALA
ERNAKULAM	Novel House School Supplies, 8792342807
	ASSAM
GUWAHATI	Central Book Agency, 9954707165
SILCHER	New Book Stall, 919435712617
JORHAT	Bajrang stationery, 9706978968
	RAJASTHAN
ANUPGARH	City Pride Departmental Store, 919414095677
BARMER	Dev Indra Enterprises, 7073282106
	MANIPUR
IMPHAL	Global Agencies, 917641814494
	PUNJAB
TARN TARAN	Sital Di Hatti, 919988206890
KHAMMAM	Sri Nivasa Book Stall, 919948247838
	CHHATTISGARH
RAIPUR	Central Book House, 9406016308

Our Distributors

	ANDHRA PRADESH
VISAKHAPA-THAM	Sri Rajeshwari Book Link, 9848036014,
VIJAYAWADA	Sree Vidya Book Depot, 9491830839
	ANDAMAN & NICOBAR ISLAND
PORTBLAIR	Krishna Book Centre, 9474205570
	ARUNACHAL PRADESH
NAHARLAGUN	New Pothi Ghar, 8731832947
	ASSAM
SILCHAR	Book Emporium, 9675972993, 6000763186,
	New Book Stall, 9435712617
GUWAHATI	Kayaan Enterprises, (0361) 2630443,
	BIHAR
PATNA	Nova Publisher & Distributors, (0612) 2666404
	Vikas Book Depot, 9504780402
	Gyan Ganga Limited, 9304826651, Rishu Pustak Bhandar, 8294576789,
	Sri Durga Pustak Mandir, 9334477386
	Bokaro Student Friends Pvt. Ltd, 7277931285
BIHAR SHARIF	Good Books , 8210685462
MUZAFFARPUR	Pustak Bhandar, 7870834225
	CHATTISGARH
AMBIKAPUR	M.P Department Stores, 9425254264
BOKARO	Bokaro Student Friends Pvt. Ltd, Bokaro, 7277931285
DURG	Bhagwati Bhawani Book Depot, 0788-2327620, 9827473100
RAIPUR	Gupta Pustak Mandir, 7974220323,
BILASPUR	Pustak Bhawan, 9300667909
	DELHI
DELHI	Mittal Books, (011) 23288887, 9899037390, A One Books, New Delhi, 8800497047,
	Batheja Super Store, 9871833924, 9811182352, Zombozone, 9871274082,
	LDS Marketing, 9811182352/9999353491, R.D. Chawla & Sons, 9810045752,
	Janta Book Depot, 9313046321
	Bokaro Student Friends Pvt. Ltd, 7004074900

	GUJARAT
AHMEDABAD	Patel Book Agencies, 9898184248, 9824386112, 9825900335,
	Shalibhadra Stationers, 9904477855
VAPI	Goutam Book Sellers, 9081790813
VADODARA	Shree ji Book Depot, 9824649375, Nilesh Book Centre, 9924458748
	Umakant Book Sellers & Stationer, 6359396370
AHMEDNAGAR	Hira Stationers, 9970150300
	HARYANA
ROHTAK	Swami Kitab Ghar, 9355611088, Babu Ram Pradeep Kumar, 9813214692
GURGAON	Book Care Centre Venture, 9654564783
REWARI	Repro Books Ltd, 8657315914, Annu book depot, 9053246268
	JHARKHAND
BOKARO	Bokaro Student Friends Pvt. Ltd. (0654) 2233094, 7360021503,
	Bharati Bhawan Agencies, 06542-265302, 9431740797
HAZARIBAGH	Khandelwal Book Depot, 9708607489
DEOGHAR	Navyug Sahitya Mandir, 9031917035
RANCHI	Crown Book Distributor & Publishers, (0651) 2213735, 9431173904,
	Pustak Mandir, 9431115138, Agarwal Book Depot, 9334869210, Jayshree Book House, 8434430311
	Bokaro Student Friends Pvt. Ltd, 7360021508
DHANBAD	Bokaro Student Friends Pvt. Ltd, 6202834756
	KARNATAKA
HUBLI	Renuka Book Distributor, (0836) 2244124,
	Vidyamandir Book Distributors, 9980773976
BANGLORE	Krishna book house, 9739847334,
	Sapna Book House Pvt. Ltd., 9980513242,
	Sree Sai Ram Book Traders, 9738881088
	MADHYA PRADESH
INDORE	Pustak Bhawan, 8982150100, Bhaiya Store, 9425318103
	S.P. & Publication, 7000025933, Bhaiya Industries, 9109120101
GWALIOR	Agarwal Book Depot, 9425116210
JABALPUR	Vinay Pustak Sadan, 8962362667,
	Anand Books and Stationers, 9425323508
	Akash Book Distributor, 8989111444, Bharat Book House, 9826541542

21/05/25

Our Distributors

KATNI	Shri Mahavir Agency, 9425363412
	MAHARASHTRA
AMRAVATI	Delta Pen House, 9890350073
PUNE	Vikas Book House, 9921331187, Pravin Sales, 9890683475,
	New Saraswati Granth Bhandar, 9422323859
	Sai Book Collection, 9623224343
	Yash Agencies, 9850956542
MUMBAI	New Student Agencies, 7045065799,
	Shivam Books & Stationery, 8619805332
LATUR	Yash Book House, 9637936999
KOLHAPUR	Jai Book Co. 9404671543
NAGPUR	Laxmi Pustakalay and Stationers, (0712) 2727354, Vijay Book Depot, 9860122094
	Renuka Book Distributor, 9765406133, Novelty Book Depot, 9657690220,
	Shree Mahalaxmi Pustakalaya, 7507099360
DHULE	Navjeevan Book Stall, 7020525561
YAVATMAL	Shri Ganesh Pustkalaya, 9423131275
VASAI	Prime Book Centre, Vasai, 9890293662
	ODISHA
CUTTACK	A. K. Mishra Agencies, 9437025991, 9437081319
BHUBANESHWAR	M/s Pragnya, 8847888616, 9437943777, Padmalaya, 9437026922,
	Bidyashree, 9937017070,
KEONJHAR	Students Corner, 7008435418
KORAPUT	Ambica Book Centre, 7008585008
	PUNJAB
AMBALA	Bharat Book Depot, 7988455354
PATIALA	Goel Sons, 9463619978,
	Adarsh Enterprises, 9814347613
JALANDHAR	Cheap Book Store, 9872223458, 9878258592, City Book Shop, 9417440753,
	Subhash Book Depot, 9876453625,
	Gaurav Book world, 9478821183
LUDHIANA	Gupta Brothers, 9888200206,
	Bhatia Book Centre, 9815277131, Amit Book Depot, 9815807871
CHANDIGARH	Mohindra Book Depot, 9814920226
BATHINDA	Goyal Sons , 9464478362, Bhagwati Book Depot, 9463120564
	RAJASTHAN
AJMER	Laxmi General Store, Ajmer, 0145- 2428942 9460652197
KOTA	Raj Traders, 9309232829
BHILWARA	Nakoda Book Depot, (01482) 243653, 9214983594,
JAIPUR	Saraswati Book House, (0141) 2610823, 9829811155,
	Goyal Book Distt., 9460983939, 9414782130
JODHPUR	Kitab Mahal, 9460957875
	TRIPURA
AGARTALA	Books Corner, 8794894165, 8984657146
	TAMIL NADU
COIMBATORE	Majestic Book House, 9791966665
	KERALA
ERNAKULAM	Academic Book House, (0484) 2376613, H & C Store, 9864196344

KOTTAYAM	Asad Book Centre, (0481) 2566992
TRIVANDRUM	Academic Book House, (0471) 2333349, 9447063349
CALICUT	Aman Book Stall, (0495) 2721282,
KOZHIKODE	T.B.S. Publishers Distributors, 7559822223
MADURAI	Selvi Book Shoppe, 9843057435
CHENNAI	M.R. Book Store (044) 25364596,
	Kalaimagal Store, (044) 5544072, 9940619404, Vijaya Stores, 9381037417,
	Bookmark It-Books & Stat. Store, 7305151653,
	M.K. Stores, 9840030099, Tiger Books Pvt. Ltd., 9710447000,
	TELANGANA
HYDERABAD	Sri Balaji Book Depot, (040) 27613300, 9866355473
	Vishal Book Distributors, 9246333166
	UTTARAKHAND
DEHRADUN	Inder Book Agencies, 9634045280
	Brothers Pustak Bhandar, 9897833882
	UTTAR PRADESH
AGRA	Sparsh Book Agency, 9412257817,
	Sanjay Publication, 8126699922 Arti book centre, 8630128856,
	Om Pustak Mandir, (0562) 2464014, 9319117771
	Panchsheel Books, 9412257962, 9412257961
	Manav Book World, 9760316933
MATHURA	Sapra Traders, 9410076716
ALLAHABAD	Mehrotra Book Agency, (0532) 2266865, 9415636890
AZAMGARH	Sasta Sahitya Bhandar, 9450029674
ALIGARH	K.B.C.L. Agarwal, 9897124960,
NAJIBABAD	Gupta News Agency, 8868932500
KANPUR	Radha News Agency, 8957247427,
	Raj Book Dist., 9235616506,
	H K Book Distributors, 9506033137/9935146730
GORAKHPUR	Vidyarthi Sahitya Bhandar, 6394026706
LUCKNOW	Om Book Depot, 7705871398, Azad Book Depot Pvt. Ltd., 7317000250,
	Ashirwad Book Depot, 9235501197, Book.com, 7458922755, Universal Books,
	9450302161, Sheetla Book Agency, 9235832418, Vidyarthi Kendra Publisher & Distributor Pvt Ltd, 9554967415, Tripathi Book House, 9415425943,
	Navyug Book Agencies, 8073564410, Pustak Vatika, 7905317119
MEERUT	Ideal Book Depot, (0121) 4059252, 9837066307
NOIDA	Goyal Books Overseas Pvt.Ltd., 1204655555, 9873387003
PRAYAGRAJ	Kanhaiya Pustak Bhawan, 9415317109
RENUKOOT	Om Stationers, 7007326732
VARANASI	Bokaro Student Friends Pvt. Ltd , 9798050654
	WEST BENGAL
KOLKATA	Oriental Publishers & Distributor (033) 40628367, Katha 'O' Kahini, (033)
	22196313, 22419071, Saha Book House, (033), 22193671, 9333416484,
	United Book House, 9831344622, Bijay Pustak Bhandar, 8961260603,
NORTH DINAJPUR	Sarkar Book Suppliers, 9830949359
COOCH BEHAR	S.B. Book Distributor, Cooch behar, 9002670771
KHARAGPUR	Subhani Book Store, 9046891334

21/05/25

CHAPTER

1 UNSEEN PASSAGES

WORKSHEET-1

Name	Class............	Roll No..........	Time 20 Min.	Max. Marks 15	Marks Obtained

1. Read the passage given below and answer the questions that follow: **(1 × 5 = 5)**

A farmer placed a net over the field that he'd just planted for catching a bunch of crows that came to eat his seeds. Caught with them was a stork that had broken its leg in the net. The stork did not want to be punished like crows so it pleaded the farmer for his freedom. The stork tried to convince the farmer that it was not like other crows, it worked for its father and mother but the farmer did not listen to him and said, "You may be as you say, but what I know is that, I caught you with thieves, and so I will treat you like a thief".

(i) Why did the farmer place net over the fields?

Ans. ....

....

(ii) For what did the stork request the farmer?

Ans. ....

(iii) How did the stork try to convince the farmer?

Ans. ....

....

....

(iv) Why did the farmer not release the stork?

Ans. ....

....

(v) Give the synonyms of 'convince' and 'pleaded'.

Ans. ....

....

2. Read the passage given below and answer the questions that follow: **(1 × 5 = 5)**

Very soon, Galileo found himself in the University. He was a strong young man with red hair and a cheerful face but was very short tempered. He often disagreed with his teachers. The professors at Pisa disliked him because he was determined to think for himself and test all the theories they taught him by practical experiments. They were content with teaching what ancient Greek philosophers had taught for so long. But as a true scientist, Galileo refused to accept any idea without questions.

(i) How did Galileo look?

Ans. ....

....

(ii) What was the weakness of Galileo?

Ans. ....

....

(iv) What showed that Galileo was a true scientist?

Ans. ....

....

....

(v) Find the word that means:

(a) To get angry very soon **(b)** Very old

Ans. ....

....

3. **Read the passage given below and answer the questions that follow:**

Once, the lion the king of the jungle, the lion said to its friend, "As you know I am the king of the jungle and my cub is going to be the next king, I want to provide him with the education that is fit for a king. Please suggest a good teacher for my cub." The owl suggested the fox, as it is supposed to be veryclever. The lion replied, "No way! The fox is very cunning and he always lies; he cannot teach my son". The owl suggested the elephant but the lion said, "the elephant is just strong but not intelligent; he cannot be my cub's teacher".

The owl suggested many animals' names but the lion did not approve anybody. Finally, the owl said, "Ok why don't I teach your son"? The lion readily agreed as the owl is supposed to be very wise. He appointed the wise owl as the cub's teacher.

Fill in the blanks with the correct option: **(1 × 5 = 5)**

(i) The young one of a lion is called a .... (cub, lioness, prince)

Ans. ....

(ii) The lion wanted a good .... for his cub. (partner, friend, teacher)

Ans. ....

(iii) He did not want the fox to teach his cub because he was .... (cunning, silly, clever)

Ans. ....

(iv) Finally the lion selected the .... as his cub's teacher. (elephant, owl, monkey)

Ans. ....

(v) The opposite of wise is .... (foolish, wisdom, intelligent)

Ans. ....

❑❑❑

UNSEEN PASSAGES

WORKSHEET-2

Name	Class............	Roll No..........	Time 20 Min.	Max. Marks 15	Marks Obtained

1. Read the passage given below and answer the questions that follow: **(1 × 5 = 5)**

During an auspicious or special occasion banana plant, complete with fruit and flower is tied to the entrance. This plant is a symbol of completeness and a prosperous family. From the point of nutrition, banana is rich in fibre and potassium. With an abundance of vitamins and minerals, banana is a healthy part of any diet.

(i) When is the banana plant tied to the entrance?

Ans. ....

....

(ii) What is a banana plant symbol of?

Ans. ....

....

(iii) From a nutritional point of view, what is a banana rich in?

Ans. ....

....

(iv) Why is banana known as the healthy part of any diet?

Ans. ....

....

(v) Find words which mean same as:

(a) Wealthy and happy

(b) Great amount

Ans. ....

....

2. Read the passage given below and answer the questions that follow: **(1 × 5 = 5)**

Cricket grew out of many stick and ball games played in England about 500 years ago. The word 'bat' is an old English word which simply means a club or a stick. By the seventeenth century, cricket had evolved enough to be recognised as a distinct game. Till the middle of the eighteenth century, bats were roughly of the same shape as hockey sticks, curving outwards at the bottom. There was a simple reason for this, the ball was bowled underarm, along the ground and the curve at the end of the bat gave the batsman the best chance of making a contact.

(i) How did the game of cricket come into being?

Ans. ....

....

(ii) What does the word 'bat' actually mean?

Ans. ....

(iii) What were the shapes of bats of the eighteenth century?

Ans. ....

....

(iv) How was the ball bowled in the eighteenth century?

Ans. ....

(v) Give the word that means the opposite of:

(a) Simple

(b) Bottom

Ans. ....

....

3. Read the passage given below and answer the questions that follow: **($1 \times 5 = 5$)**

National Anthems are sung or played on special occasions in almost all the countries of the world. They are patriotic songs, sung as a mark of honour to the countries concerned. These are sung to inspire patriotic feelings in people. It is believed that 'Kim Gao' song sung in Japan, was the first national anthem of the world. Our national anthem was written by Rabindra Nath Tagore and was sung for the first time at Kolkata session of the Congress in 1911. On 24th January 1950, it was adopted as the national anthem of India. 'Vande-Matram', a patriotic song written by Bankim Chandra Chatterjee has also been given the status almost similar to that of national anthem.

(i) What is national anthem?

Ans. ....

....

(ii) When is national anthem sung?

Ans. ....

(iii) Who wrote our national anthem and when was it adopted?

Ans. ....

....

....

(iv) Which song is given almost equal status as national anthem?

Ans. ....

....

(v) Find words which mean the same:

(a) Respect

(b) Love for country

Ans. ....

....

❑❑❑

CHAPTER

1 UNSEEN PASSAGES

WORKSHEET-3

Name	Class.............	Roll No..........	Time 20 Min.	Max. Marks 15	Marks Obtained

1. Read the passage given below and answer the questions that follow: **(1 × 5 = 5)**

Once a greedy man had a goose that laid a golden egg everyday. He sold the golden egg in the market. This made him very rich. His greed increased day by day. After sometime he said to himself, "My goose lay one egg in a day. That gives me seven eggs in a week. That is a very slow process. I will kill it and get all the golden eggs at once". So he foolishly killed the goose. There was no gold in her body. All the goose are the same. The greedy man wept and repented for his foolishness. He said, "Oh! I have lost all with my greed".

(i) What did the goose lay daily?

Ans. ....

(ii) How did the man become rich?

Ans. ....

....

(iii) According to the man what was the slow process?

Ans. ....

....

(iv) Why did he kill the goose?

Ans. ....

....

(v) Find the opposites of:

(a) Decreased

(b) Wisely

Ans. ....

....

2. Read the passage given below and answer the questions that follow: **(1 × 5 = 5)**

A camel and a jackal were friends. One day, the jackal took his friend to a big sugarcane farm. It was on the opposite side of the river. After a sumptuous meal the jackal began to howl loudly. The camel pleaded jackal not to do so, but jackal said that it was his habit. Soon the farmers came and thrashed the camel badly. When the camel crossed the river, the jackal joined him on his back. The camel took deliberate dip into the water. When the jackal pleaded, the camel said that he had the habit of rolling in the water after every meal. The poor jackal was drowned.

(i) Where did jackal take camel one day?

Ans. ....

(ii) Why did the farmers thrash the camel?

Ans. ....

....

(iii) How did the camel take his revenge on jackal?

Ans. ....

....

(iv) What was the end of jackal?

Ans. ....

(v) Give the synonym of 'sumptuous' and 'thrashed'.

Ans. ....

....

3. Read the passage given below and answer the questions that follow: **(1 × 5 = 5)**

India is the largest country in South-East Asia. India has very high mountains in the North, called Himalayas. It is surrounded by the Arabian Sea in the West, the Bay of Bengal in the East and the Indian Ocean in the South. India has various types of climates. The climate on the Himalayan mountains is cold and wet. The southern part of India is hot. The capital of India is New Delhi. The Indian national flag has three colours and is called the Tricolour or Tiranga.

(i) Which are the very high mountains of India and where are they located?

Ans. ....

....

(ii) By what is India surrounded on three sides?

Ans. ....

....

(iii) Name the capital of India.

Ans. ....

....

(iv) Why is the Indian national flag called 'Tiranga'?

Ans. ....

....

(v) Find the opposite from the passage of the following:

(a) Smallest

(b) Dry

Ans. ....

....

❑❑❑

UNSEEN PASSAGES

WORKSHEET-4

Name	Class............	Roll No..........	Time 20 Min.	Max. Marks 15	Marks Obtained

1. Read the passage given below and answer the questions that follow: (1 × 5 = 5)

Agnes Bojakhiu was born in Skopje, Yugoslavia of Albanian parents. Her father was a prosperous merchant. She was attracted to the life of missionary in India at a very early age. At eighteen, taking the name of Teresa in the memory of Little Flower of Lisieux, she entered the Missionary Order of the Loreto Sisters and on January 20, 1931, she stepped off a steamship onto the quay at Calcutta, then the largest city in the Empire after London. For sixteen years, she taught Geography to the daughters of well-to-do British and Bengali society in one of the most prestigious convents in Calcutta. One day in 1946, however, during a train journey to Darjeeling, a town on the slopes of the Himalayas, she heard a voice. God was asking her to leave the comfort of her convent, to go and live among the poorest of the poor in the vast city beyond. Having first obtained the permission from the Pope, she changed into a plain white cotton sari and founded a new religious order whose vocation was to relieve the misery of the most neglected of men. In 1950, the Order of the Missionaries of Charity was born, a congregation which thirty-five years later would have two hundred and eighty-five thousand charitable foundations throughout India and all the other continents, including countries behind the Iron Curtain.

(Source : 'The City of Joy' by Dominique Lapierre)

Complete the following sentences on the basis of your reading of the passage:

(i) Mother Teresa was formerly called ....

Ans. ....

(ii) After joining the Missionary Order of the Loreto Sisters, Teresa ....

Ans. ....

....

(iii) Mother Teresa left the comforts of the convent because ....

Ans. ....

....

(iv) Mother Teresa headed the Missionaries of Charity, whose aim was ....

Ans. ....

....

(v) Find out words from the passage which have the same meaning as:

(a) A person's trade or profession **(b)** Successful

Ans. ....

....

2. Read the passage given below and answer the questions that follow: (1 × 5 = 5)

'Health is wealth' is a well known saying. Without good health, life is a burden. When we fall ill, we are unhappy. We cannot work or play. Germs cause illness. These are very small living things. They live on dirt and grow in darkness. They get into our body by air, water, food or cuts in the skin and make us ill. Dirt and darkness are the enemies of a good health. They breed germs. Sunlight and cleanliness destroy them. So we must keep our body clean and do exercise daily to keep ourselves healthy. Bad habits like smoking and drinking alcohol must be avoided.

(i) What happens when we fall ill?

Ans. ....

(ii) What are germs and where do they live?

Ans. ....

....

(iii) How do germs enter our body?

Ans. ....

....

(iv) What should we do to keep good health?

Ans. ....

....

(v) Find the opposites of:

(a) Friends (b) Bad

Ans. ....

....

3. **Read the passage given below and answer the questions that follow:** **(1 × 5 = 5)**

Gorelal was a famous sculptor. His sculptures looked like real ones. One day, he saw a dream that after fifteen days, the demon of death would come to take him. Gorelal prepared nine statues of himself and on the fifteenth day, when the demon of death was to come, he took his place among the statues. The demon could not recognise him and was astonished to see ten Gorelals instead of one. He returned without taking him. Now the God of death came himself. He was also confused so he said, "Gorelal these sculptures would have been perfect but for one mistake", Gorelal could not tolerate the fault finding in his work. He came out and asked, "Where is the fault"? God of death caught him and said, "Here". His pride made his fall.

(i) How did the sculptures of Gorelal look?

Ans. ....

....

(ii) What did Gorelal dream one day?

Ans. ....

....

(iii) What did Gorelal do after the dream?

Ans. ....

....

(iv) How was Gorelal caught by the God of death?

Ans. ....

....

....

....

(v) Give the synonyms of 'astonished' and 'caught'.

Ans. ....

....

❑❑❑

CHAPTER

1 UNSEEN PASSAGES

WORKSHEET-5

Name	Class.............	Roll No..........	Time 20 Min.	Max. Marks 15	Marks Obtained

1. **Read the passage given below:** **(1 × 5 = 5)**

He (the convict) asked me where my father and mother were. When I had pointed out their tombstones to him; he asked me with whom I lived. I told him that I lived with my sister, wife of Joe Gargery, the black-smith.

On hearing the word 'black-smith' he looked down at his legs and then at me. He took me by both arms and ordered me to bring him early the next morning, a file and some food, or he would have my heart and liver out. I was not to say a word about it at all. "I am not alone," he said, "as you may think I am. There is a youngman hidden within me in comparison with whom I am an angel. That youngman hears the words I speak. That young man has a secret way, peculiar to himself, of getting at a boy, and at his heart and at his liver. It is in vain for a boy to attempt to hide himself from the youngman".

I promised to bring him the file, and what broken bits of food I could, and wished him good night. He limped towards the low church wall, got over it, and then turned round to look for me. When I saw him turning, I set my face towards home and made the best use of my legs. (Philip, called Pip, is the speaker.)

Complete the following sentences on the basis of your reading of the passage:

(i) The speaker lived with Joe Gargery and his sister because...

Ans. ....

(ii) If the speaker did not bring a file and food for the convict, he...

Ans. ....

(iii) The convict's threat to the speaker was..

Ans. ....

(iv) Before bidding the convict good night, the speaker promised that...

Ans. ....

(v) Find out words from the passage which have the same meaning as:

(a) Strange **(b)** Useless

Ans. ....

....

2. **Read the passage given below:** **(1 × 5 = 5)**

The great defect of our civilisation is that it does not know what to do with its knowledge. Science has given us power fit for the God, yet we use it like small children. For example, we do not know how to manage our machines. Machines were made to be man's servants; yet he had grown so dependent upon them that they in a fair way have become his master. Already, most men spend most of their lives looking after and waiting upon machines. And the machines are very stern master. They must be fed with coal and petrol to drink, and oil to wash with, and they must be kept at the right temperature. And if they do not get their meals when they expect them, they grow sulky and refuse to work, or burst with rage, and blow up, and spread ruin and destruction all around them. So we have to wait upon them very attentively and do all that we can, to keep them in good temper. Already we find it difficult either to work or play without the machines, and a time may come when they will rule us altogether just as we rule animals.

And this brings me to the point at which I asked, "What do we do with all the time which the machines have saved for us, and the new energy they have given us? On the whole it must be admitted, we do very little. For the most part we use our time and energy to make more and better machines; but more and better machines will only give us still more time and still more energy, and what we are to do with them"? The answer, I think, is that we should try to become more civilised. For the machines themselves, and the power which the machines have given us, are no civilisation but aids to civilisation. *(C.M. Joad)*

Complete the following sentences on the basis of your reading of the passage:

(i) Our civilisation is defective because...

Ans. ....

(ii) If the machines are not properly looked after and kept fully satisfied.......................................

Ans. ....

(iii) A time is soon expected to come when...

Ans. ....

(iv) The best way to use the additional time and energy, that machines have given to us is.....................

Ans. ....

(v) Write the meaning of this sentence in simple words: 'Science has given us power, fit for the God, yet we use them like small children'.

Ans. ....

3. Read the passage given below and answer the questions that follow:

I came in contact with animals far more in prison than outside. I had always been fond of dogs and had kept some but I could never look after them properly as other matters claimed my attention. In prison, I was grateful for their company. Indians do not, as a rule, approve of the animals as household pets. It is remarkable that inspite of their general philosophy of non-violence to animals, they are often singularly careless and unkind towards them. Even the cow, the favoured animal, though looked up to and almost worshipped by many Hindus, becomes often the cause of riots, fit is not treated kindly. Worship and kindliness do not always go together.

Different countries have adopted different animals as a symbol of their ambition or character — the eagle of the United States of America and of Germany, the lion and bulldog of England, the fighting cock of France, the bear of old Russia. How far do these patron animals mould national character? Most of them are aggressive, fighting animals, beasts of prey. It is not surprising that the people who grow up with these examples before them should mould themselves consciously after them and strike up aggressive attitudes, and roar and prey on others. Nor is it surprising that the Hindu should be mild and non-violent, for his patron animal is the cow. *(Jawahar Lal Nehru)*

Complete the following sentences on the basis of your reading of the passage: **(1 × 5 = 5)**

(i) The author could not take care of his pets because.....................

Ans. ....

(ii) An example to show that worship and kindliness do not always go together is.....................

Ans. ....

....

(iii) People from countries who have adopted fighting animals as their national symbol develop violence in their attitude because ....

Ans. ....

....

(iv) Since, the patron animal of the Hindus is the cow, it is not surprising that ....

Ans. ....

(v) Find out words from the passage which have the same meaning as:

(a) Ready to attack **(b)** Strong desire to achieve

Ans. ....

....

❑❑❑

SHORT & LONG WRITING TASKS

WORKSHEET-6

Name	Class..............	Roll No..........	Time 25 Min.	Max. Marks 18	Marks Obtained

1. Write an application to your Principal asking him to grant you leave for a week as you are not well and the doctor has advised you to take rest. You are Rohita, a student of Class VII of MPS Public School, Rajkot. **(6)**

Ans. ....

....

....

....

....

....

....

....

....

....

....

....

....

....

....

....

....

....

....

....

2. Write an application to the Principal of your school asking him to grant you three days leave, as you have to go to Delhi to attend your brother's wedding. You are Sumit, a student of class VII of K.D. Public School, Agra. **(6)**

Ans. ....

....

....

....

....

3. You are Rupak of K. D. Public School, Agra. Write an application to your Principal for allowing you to attend the school in civil dress for a few days as the uniform of your size is not available. **(6)**

Ans.

❑❑❑

SHORT & LONG WRITING TASKS WORKSHEET-7

Name	Class..............	Roll No..........	Time 25 Min.	Max. Marks 18	Marks Obtained

1. You are Kartik, a student of class VII of Life Line Public School, Faridabad. Write an application to the Principal of your school to change your section. **(6)**

Ans. ....

....

....

....

....

....

....

....

....

....

....

....

....

....

....

....

....

....

....

....

....

2. You are Suyash of Saraswati Vidya Mandir, Kota. Write an application to your Principal asking him to start evening games in your school. **(6)**

Ans. ....

....

....

....

....

....

....

3. You are Yogesh of Sarvodaya Bal Vidya Mandir, Trilokpuri, Delhi. Write an application to your Principal, requesting him to arrange for extra classes of English as your teacher is on a one-month leave. **(6)**

Ans.

❑❑❑

SHORT & LONG WRITING TASKS WORKSHEET-8

Name	Class..............	Roll No..........	Time 20 Min.	Max. Marks 18	Marks Obtained

1. You are Akansha, a student of Smith Public School, Bareilly. Write a letter to the librarian in your school, asking her to issue a new library card to you as you are new to the school. **(6)**

Ans. ....

2. Write an application to the Principal of your school asking him to arrange for some more Tablas and Sitars for the school music room. You are Kirti of Navodaya Public School, Ajmer. **(6)**

Ans. ....

3. You are Paras of R. K. Public School, Kanpur studying in Class VII. Write an application to the Principal of your school, asking him to change your name in the school records. **(6)**

Ans.

❑❑❑

SHORT & LONG WRITING TASKS — WORKSHEET-9

Name	Class.............	Roll No..........	Time 25 Min.	Max. Marks 18	Marks Obtained

1. You are Amit Kumar and you live at 354 Rose Gardens, Bangalore. You have heard that a Talent Search competition is to be held shortly in your city. Write an application to the District Education Officer, Bangalore, expressing your desire to participate in the competition. **(6)**

Ans. ....

2. You are Rajat Mittal of Sarvodaya Senior Secondary School, Vikas Nagar, Delhi. You do not have the facility of learning computers in your school. Write a letter to the Principal of your school requesting him to provide the facility to the students of the class. **(6)**

Ans. ....

3. You are Salman of Ansari Public School, Aligarh. Write an application to the Principal of your school asking him to permit you to avail bus facility from the month of August. **(6)**

Ans.

SHORT & LONG WRITING TASKS WORKSHEET-10

Name	Class.............	Roll No..........	Time 20 Min.	Max. Marks 12	Marks Obtained

1. Write a letter to the Chairman of your Municipality, complaining about the insanitary condition of the locality in which you live and asking him to take necessary steps in this matter. **(6)**

Ans. ....

2. Write a letter to the Editor 'Nav Bharat Times, New Delhi' showing your concern about unauthorised encroachment on roads and market-places. **(6)**

Ans. ....

❑❑❑

SHORT & LONG WRITING TASKS WORKSHEET-11

Name	Class..............	Roll No..........	Time 20 Min.	Max. Marks 12	Marks Obtained

1. Write a letter to the Editor of the Times of India regarding the nuisance of stray animals/dogs on the roads of your colony. Sign yourself as Subhash/Kirti of Malviya Nagar, New Delhi. **(6)**

Ans. ....

2. Write a letter to the postmaster complaining against the irregular delivery of your letters. You are Amit/ Anita, a resident of Janakpuri, New Delhi. **(6)**

Ans.

❑❑❑

SHORT & LONG WRITING TASKS WORKSHEET-12

Name	Class..............	Roll No..........	Time 20 Min.	Max. Marks 12	Marks Obtained

1. Write a letter to your friend thanking him for a lovely holiday you spent at his house in Mumbai. **(6)**

Ans. ....

2. You are Rohit and you stay in R.K. Residency Hostel, Udaipur. Write a letter to your mother that you have made new friends there and how you are enjoying your life. **(6)**

Ans. ....

❑❑❑

CHAPTER

2 SHORT & LONG WRITING TASKS

WORKSHEET-13

Name	Class..............	Roll No..........	Time 20 Min.	Max. Marks 12	Marks Obtained

1. You are Shubham of 36, Lajpat Nagar, New Delhi. Write a letter to your friend asking him to suggest you the names of some good story books that you should read. **(6)**

Ans. ....

2. Write a letter to your friend Akshay telling him how you celebrated your birthday this year. You are Karan of Kanpur. **(6)**

Ans. ....

❑❑❑

SHORT & LONG WRITING TASKS WORKSHEET-14

Name	Class..............	Roll No..........	Time 20 Min.	Max. Marks 12	Marks Obtained

1. Write a letter to your friend Kavish thanking him for the birthday present he sent you. You are Raghav from Chennai. **(6)**

Ans. ....

2. Write a letter to your friend Kamal staying in Delhi, telling him about the one day picnic you went for with your schoolmates. You are Rohan from Agra. **(6)**

Ans. ....

❑❑❑

SHORT & LONG WRITING TASKS WORKSHEET-15

Name	Class..............	Roll No..........	Time 20 Min.	Max. Marks 16	Marks Obtained

1. Write a short composition on 'My Family'. **(4)**

Ans. ....

2. Write a short composition on 'Independence Day'. **(4)**

Ans. ....

3. Write a short composition on 'My Favourite Game'. **(4)**

Ans. ....

4. Write a short composition on 'Importance of Trees'. **(4)**

Ans.

SHORT & LONG WRITING TASKS

WORKSHEET-16

Name	Class............	Roll No..........	Time 20 Min.	Max. Marks 16	Marks Obtained

1. Write a short composition on 'A Visit to a Zoo'. **(4)**

Ans. ....

2. Write a short composition on 'My Neighbour'. **(4)**

Ans. ....

3. Write a short composition on 'My Favourite Book'. **(4)**

Ans.

4. Write a short composition on 'My School'. **(4)**

Ans.

❑❑❑

SHORT & LONG WRITING TASKS WORKSHEET-17

Name	Class.............	Roll No..........	Time 20 Min.	Max. Marks 16	Marks Obtained

1. Write a short composition on 'Computer'. **(4)**

Ans. ....

....

....

....

....

....

....

....

....

....

....

....

....

2. Write a short composition on 'Importance of Sports and Games'. **(4)**

Ans. ....

....

....

....

....

....

....

....

....

....

....

....

....

....

....

3. Write a short composition on 'Republic Day'. (4)

Ans. ....

4. **Write a composition on 'My best friend' using the hints given.** (4)

We all have friends whom we like to share things with. But one of them is our best friend. With the help of the hints given tell us something about your best friend.

Hints: Who is your friend? How do you know him? How do you spend time together?

Ans. ....

❑❑❑

SHORT & LONG WRITING TASKS WORKSHEET-18

Name	Class..............	Roll No..........	Time 20 Min.	Max. Marks 16	Marks Obtained

1. Write a composition on 'My Pet' using the hints given. **(4)**

Humans and animals have always been in close contact with each other. A lot of people keep pet animals. Write something about your pet animal using the hints given.

Hints : What animal is your pet ? What does it do '*Hints:*'? What do you do for it?

Ans. ....

....

....

....

....

....

....

....

....

....

....

2. Write a composition on 'Uses and abuses of mobile phones' using the hints given. **(4)**

Today mobile phones have become a very common thing and they can be found in the hands of everyone. But everything has two sides—one good and the other bad. Use the hints given below and develop a paragraph.

Hints: Connects people- makes fast contacts- distracts students- waste time on it.

Ans. ....

....

....

....

....

....

....

....

....

....

....

....

....

....

3. Write a composition on 'The person I admire that most' using the hints given. **(4)**

In our daily life we meet a lot of people or come to know about them. Some of them we like and some we don't. On the basis of the hints write a composition.

Hints: Who is the person? How do you know him? What do you like about that person?

Ans. ....

....

....

....

....

....

....

....

....

....

....

....

4. Write a composition on 'Gifts of Science' using the hints given. **(4)**

Science has given us a lot of things which have become a part of our life. Use the hints given below and share your views about it.

Hints: What all science has given? How is it useful?

Ans. ....

....

....

....

....

....

....

....

....

....

....

❑❑❑

WORKSHEET-19

Name	Class..............	Roll No...........	Time 10 Min.	Max. Marks 4	Marks Obtained

1. Write a composition on the following picture: **(4)**

A birthday party means a lot of fun. Do you think these kids are having fun? Write a short composition on it.

Ans. ....

❑❑❑

SHORT & LONG WRITING TASKS WORKSHEET-20

Name	Class..............	Roll No..........	Time 10 Min.	Max. Marks 4	Marks Obtained

1. Write a composition on the following picture: **(4)**

What do you think the children in the picture are doing and what they are learning?

Ans. ....

....

....

....

....

....

....

....

....

....

....

....

....

....

....

....

....

....

❑❑❑

SHORT & LONG WRITING TASKS WORKSHEET-21

Name	Class..............	Roll No..........	Time 15 Min.	Max. Marks 10	Marks Obtained

1. On the occasion of World Health Day, write an article in about 150 words for the school news-letter on the topic, 'Importance of Physical Health in Our Lives', using the clues given below. **(5)**

Hints:
- Healthy mind lives in a healthy body.
- Lack of time for physical activity because of the demands of modern lives.
- Ignoring the health increases the risk of many diseases,
- Discipline is the key to resolving these concerns.

Ans. ....

....

....

....

....

....

....

....

....

....

....

....

....

....

....

....

....

....

....

....

....

....

....

....

2. You are Rekha/Rohit. You have seen the following news item in a newspaper. **(5)**

> Video games. Internet, cell phones and other high-tech gadgets are just part of growing up in a digital world. But parents are concerned about the amount of time their children spend with these gadgets and worry that it might be distracting them and cramping their academic and social development.

Using your own ideas and those taken from the unit, 'Science', write an article in about 150 words describing both the benefits and drawbacks of using these high-tech devices.

OR

While reading a science journal, you came across an interesting write-up on the impact of science on our lives. A short excerpt from the write-up is given below:

> **Science—A Boon Or Bane**
>
> The advancements in science and technology have both positive and negative effects on human life. Most of the people think that there are more advantages of science and technology as compared to the disadvantages. The major advantage of science and technology is that it has made our lives easier. If technology has made our lives comfortable then it has also increased anxiety in our lives. For instance the mobile phone and the internet. Based on your understanding and using ideas from the unit 'Science' write an article for your school magazine in about 150 words on how science has an impact on our life style.

Ans. ....

❑❑❑

CHAPTER 2

SHORT & LONG WRITING TASKS WORKSHEET-22

Name	Class..............	Roll No..........	Time 15 Min.	Max. Marks 10	Marks Obtained

1. You are Shantanu/Shikha. Taking help from the picture given below and using your own ideas, write an article for the school magazine on the topic 'Saving our Earth'. (150 words) **(5)**

Ans. ....

2. Write an article to be published in your school magazine expressing your concern over the health hazards caused by fast food in about 150 words. **(5)**

Ans. ....

❑❑❑

SHORT & LONG WRITING TASKS WORKSHEET-23

Name	Class..............	Roll No..........	Time 15 Min.	Max. Marks 8	Marks Obtained

1. You are Varun Kapoor, Head Boy of J.D. Public School, Agra. The school is going to host an Inter-School English Debate competition. Write a notice calling for a meeting of members of the concerned council to discuss the arrangements to be made for the competition. **(4)**

Ans. ....

2. You are Sanjeev Ahuja, Head Boy of S.S. Public School, Agra. Draft a notice to be put on the school notice board for inviting the students to submit the articles for the school magazine to Mr. John Paul, Head of English Department. **(4)**

Ans. ....

❑❑❑

SHORT & LONG WRITING TASKS WORKSHEET-24

Name	Class..............	Roll No..........	Time 20 Min.	Max. Marks 16	Marks Obtained

1. You are Rohit, Head Boy / Rashi, Head Girl of Indian National School. Draft a notice for school notice board informing the students about the poster making competition on 'Mothers Day' in your school. Give all the necessary details of the contest and invite them to participate. **(4)**

Ans. ....

....

....

....

....

....

....

....

....

....

....

....

....

....

2. You are Shivani Gupta, Head Girl of Happy Days School, Indore. Write a notice for the school notice board informing the students about the Blood Donation Camp to be held by Blue Cross Society. **(4)**

Ans. ....

....

....

....

....

....

....

....

....

....

....

....

3. You are Sarthak Jain, a student of Class VII of Vidya Niketan School, Pune. You have lost your important documents in the school premises yesterday. Draft a notice in not more than 50 words to be put the school notice board. Finder of the documents will be suitably rewarded. **(4)**

Ans. ....

4. You are the secretary of the 'Cultural Club' of your school. The club has decided to organise a tour to visit places of historical importance in Jaipur. Write a notice in about 50 words informing the students about the tour. Give all the relevant details. **(4)**

Ans. ....

❑❑❑

SHORT & LONG WRITING TASKS WORKSHEET-25

Name	Class..............	Roll No..........	Time 20 Min.	Max. Marks 15	Marks Obtained

1. There was a storm brewing outside and you were all alone at home. Suddenly, the lights went off.......In about 80 words, write a story. You could use some of the phrases given below: **(5)**

- jumped in fright
- screamed in horror
- to my relief
- disappeared in a flash
- scared the daylight out of me
- touched something eerie.

Ans. ....

....

....

....

....

....

....

....

....

....

....

....

....

....

....

....

....

....

....

....

2. Given below is the beginning of a story. Complete it in about 80 words. **(5)**

Outline : Ravi was travelling by train—suddenly the train stopped—some stranger looking men entered the compartment—approaching from both the directions—platform was swarming with police—come to catch a terrorist.

Ans. ....

....

3. Given below is the outline of a story, develop an interesting story based on the outline. (80 words) **(5)**

Outline : Old lion—always hungry—four friends in forest—lion sees them—says he's hungry and wants to eat them—animals scared—Hare cleverest of all—tells lions about another lion—takes him to well—lion sees his reflection—Thinks another lion—roars at him—reflection roars back, lion jumps into the well—end of lion—friends happy.

Ans.

❑❑❑

SHORT & LONG WRITING TASKS WORKSHEET-26

Name	Class............	Roll No..........	Time 15 Min.	Max. Marks 10	Marks Obtained

1. Write a diary entry on your visit to a historical monument. **(5)**

Ans. ....

2. Write a diary entry on how you celebrated "Helpers Day" in your school. (5)

Ans. ....

SHORT & LONG WRITING TASKS WORKSHEET-27

Name	Class..............	Roll No...........	Time 20 Min.	Max. Marks 12	Marks Obtained

1. From options A, B, C and D, choose the form that best fits the stated function to complete the dialogue below. **(3)**

Wife : If you don't hurry, we'll be late for the show.

Husband : There's a plenty of time. ....(i).................

Why are you in a hurry? (A) It's only six O'clock (B)

I won't take long (C) You are always so impatient (D)

Wife : Plenty of time? The show starts in twenty minutes.

Husband : It takes only ten minutes to get there. We can leave now.

Wife : ....(ii).................

Good (A) That's better (B) Thank God for that! (C) It's about time! (D)

Husband : ....(iii)................. It's bad for health to be so anxious about everything.

Slow down (A) Don't worry (B) You must be patient (C) You need to relax a bit more (D)

Ans. (i)..(ii)..(iii)..

2. From options A, B, C and D, choose the form that best fits the stated function to complete the dialogue below. **(3)**

Rita : Hello, Sita Did you have a good trip?

Sita : It was not too bad. Infact I managed to sleep a bit. ....(i)..................

It was so quiet (A) The passengers slept (B)

The seat was really comfortable (C) It has made me feel rested. (D)

Rita : Is that all your luggage?

Vicky : Yes. Wait a minute. The small holdall is missing. ....(ii).................. I must have left it at the duty-free shop.

Oh dear! (A) What a nuisance! (B) Where could it be? (C) I remember now. (D)

Rita : ....(iii).................. We can ask the security guard to get it. Which shop was it?

Don't cry (A) Don't worry (B) Are you sure? (C) We'll look for it. (D)

Ans. (i)..(ii)..(iii)..

3. **From options A, B, C and D, choose the form that best fits the stated function to complete the dialogue below.** **(3)**

Ricky : Why did you give money to that beggar?

Vicky : ....(i).................. I can't walk away, ignoring him.

Why shouldn't I?	He's always there	I dislike beggars	I feel sorry for him
(A)	(B)	(C)	(D)

Ricky : You are just encouraging him to be lazy. It is a bad habit.

Vicky : He looks old and sick.

Ricky : ....(ii).................. but there are organizations to help people like him.

All right	Yes, he does	I believe you,	You may be right
(A)	(B)	(C)	(D)

Vicky : And what are they doing to help him?

Ricky : All right ....(iii)..................

Let's go	Forget it	Do what you like	Let's not argue about it.
(A)	(B)	(C)	(D)

Ans. (i)..(ii)..(iii)..

4. **From options A, B, C and D, choose the form that best fits the stated function to complete the dialogue below.** **(3)**

Sonu : Monu, I'm having a get-together in my house on Wednesday night .... (i)...........

Are you free?	Would you like to come?
(A)	(B)
I'm sure you'd like to come	If you come, you'll enjoy yourself.
(C)	(D)

Monu : I'm sorry Sonu. I won't be able to come. I promised my mother that I will have dinner with her on Wednesday night.

Sonu : ....(ii).................. How is your mother by the way?

Take it easy	You're welcome	That's all right	I don't mind
(A)	(B)	(C)	(D)

Monu : She's fine, thanks. She often asks me about you.

Sonu : ....(iii)..................

Give her my regards	I hope to see her soon
(A)	(B)
Tell her that I appreciate it	Tell her that I asked about her too
(C)	(D)

Ans. (i)..(ii)..(iii)..

❑❑❑

GRAMMAR

WORKSHEET-28

Name	Class..............	Roll No..........	Time 25 Min.	Max. Marks 20	Marks Obtained

I. Read the following sentences and mark as Assertive, Interrogative, Imperative or Exclamatory. (½ × 10 =5)

1. Are you well now?
2. May God bless you!
3. Do they keep dogs?
4. Let us enjoy bathing.
5. Bhavna, open the door.
6. The elephant is a big animal.
7. What a pleasant weather!
8. Keep quiet.
9. Why were you absent yesterday give backspace?
10. The earth moves around the sun.

Ans. 1. ....

2. ....

3. ....

4. ....

5. ....

6. ....

7. ....

8. ....

9. ....

10. ....

II. Read the following sentences and mark whether Assertive, Interrogative, Imperative or Exclamatory. (½ × 10 =5)

1. Do you drink milk daily?
2. Stars are twinkling in the sky.
3. Ah ! What a lovely rose.
4. Let us go for a river bath.
5. Let us go to the river to swim.
6. The train is not running on time.
7. Where has Rohan gone?
8. Call in the doctor please.
9. Kindly lend me your book.
10. I like this book.

Ans. 1. ....

2. ....

3. ....

4. ....

5. ....

6. ....

7. ....

8. ....

9. ....

10. ....

III. Arrange the words in each word group in a proper order so that it makes complete sense : (½ × 10 =5)

1. a my is teacher mother.
2. very is today it cold.
3. under the table cat is the.
4. the dog boy the barked at.
5. test gave us the teacher a.
6. Jill up a hill went Jack and.
7. lost my has been pen.
8. a sum easy very is this.
9. Two we are brothers.
10. The corner is the chair in.

Ans. 1. ....

2. ....

3. ....

4. ....

5. ....

6. ....

7. ....

8. ....

9. ....

10. ....

IV. Write the following sentences correctly by placing the words in the proper order. (½ × 10 =5)

1. She did we expected as.
2. He has work a hand in.
3. Mind own business your.
4. Do your what say parents.
5. What a picture beautiful!
6. At the door there is a man.
7. Dishonesty a man's career ruins.
8. Rajni of our class is the monitor.
9. The girl playing toys with her is.
10. Narendra Modi chosen was Prime-Minister as of India the.

Ans. 1. ....

2. ....

3. ....

4. ....

5. ....

6. ....

7. ....

8. ....

9. ....

10. ....

....

❑❑❑

GRAMMAR

WORKSHEET-29

Name	Class..............	Roll No..........	Time 25 Min.	Max. Marks 20	Marks Obtained

I. Write the name of: **(1 × 5 = 5)**

(1) Four Proper Nouns
(2) Four Common Nouns
(3) Four Material Nouns
(4) Four Abstract Nouns
(5) Four Collective Nouns

Ans. 1. ....

2. ....

3. ....

4. ....

5. ....

II. Supply a suitable collective noun for the following: **(½ × 10 = 5)**

1. An .... of soldiers
2. A .... of ships
3. A .... of flowers
4. A .... of lions
5. A .... of keys
6. A .... of fish
7. A .... of wolves
8. A .... of birds
9. A .... of players
10. A .... of chickens

Ans. 1. .... **2.** ....

3. .... **4.** ....

5. .... **6.** ....

7. .... **8.** ....

9. .... **10.** ....

III. Give the Abstract Nouns formed from the following words: **(½ × 10 = 5)**

1. sweet
2. humble
3. kind
4. cruel
5. live
6. think
7. man
8. friend
9. Beautiful
10. healthy

Ans. 1. .... **2.** ....

3. .... **4.** ....

5. .... **6.** ....

7. .... **8.** ....

9. .... **10.** ....

IV. Write the nouns in the following sentences and also state their types. (½ × 10 = 5)

1. The train stopped at the station.
2. A pack of cards is kept on the table.
3. The Taj Mahal is a beautiful building.
4. This necklace is made of gold.
5. The fireman could not put out the fire.
6. My family is going to Lucknow.
7. The Ganga is a holy river.
8. Many new plants have been planted in the garden.
9. The shepherd took his flock of sheep to the grassland.
10. A crowd gathered around the injured man.

Ans. ....

....

....

....

....

....

....

....

....

....

....

....

....

....

....

....

....

....

....

....

....

....

❑❑❑

WORKSHEET-30

Name	Class...............	Roll No...........	Time 30 Min.	Max. Marks 25	Marks Obtained

I. Give the singular forms of the verbs: **(½ × 10 = 5)**

Sheep, oxen, mice, branches, churches, trees, knives, mangoes, hair, stars.

Ans. **Plural** **Singular**

Plural	Singular
....	....
....	....
....	....
....	....
....	....
....	....
....	....
....	....
....	....
....	....

II. Change the following sentences from plural to singular: **(1 × 5 = 5)**

1. The women were working in the fields.
2. The babies were crying in their cradles.
3. Mangoes are kept on the tables.
4. Lions live in caves.
5. Mothers love their children.

Ans. ....

....

....

....

....

III. Change these sentences into plural form. Make the other necessary changes also: **(1 × 5 = 5)**

1. A tiger is a wild animal.
2. The doctor asked the patient to lie down.
3. The black car had no owner.
4. The policeman caught the thief.
5. A duck is swimming in the pond.

Ans. ....

....

....

....

....

IV. Change the number of the bold words: (½ × 10 = 5)

1. **A child** is playing with **a ball**.
2. **A duck** swims in water.
3. I write with **a pencil**.
4. **A mango** is kept on the table.
5. My **teeth** are aching.
6. **Dogs** are pet **animals**.
7. **Parrots** are kept as **pets**.
8. A **lion** lives in a **cave**.
9. **Mothers** love their **children**.
10. I want **a bat** and **a ball**.

Ans. ....

....

....

....

....

....

....

....

....

....

....

V. Give the plural form of the following words: (½ × 10 = 5)

Lady, box, brush, buffalo, cliff, story, flower, monkey, food, leaf.

Ans.

Plural	**Singular**
....	....
....	....
....	....
....	....
....	....
....	....
....	....
....	....
....	....
....	....

❑❑❑

GRAMMAR

WORKSHEET-31

Name	Class..............	Roll No..........	Time 30 Min.	Max. Marks 25	Marks Obtained

I. Rewrite the following sentences, changing the gender of the nouns and making other necessary changes: **(1 × 10 = 10)**

1. He owns a colt, a goose and a bull.
2. The wife is a maidservant to the queen.
3. He went with his step-son, brother-in-law and uncle to see the fair.
4. The huntress killed a tigress, a lioness and a hen.
5. The bride was thirty years old.
6. May I come in, Sir?
7. He keeps bitches and foxes.
8. He is an old bachelor.
9. The lion is the king of the forest.
10. A duck is smaller than a goose.

Ans. ....

....

....

....

....

....

....

....

....

....

....

....

....

....

....

II. Rewrite the following sentences changing the gender of the nouns and making other necessary changes: **(1 × 15 = 15)**

1. His mother took him to the zoo where he had a look at the lions, tigers, stags, rams, and peacocks.
2. The merchant accompanied by his wife and daughters came to the king's palace.
3. The poet, the priest, and the prophet are always inspired by a high ideal.
4. The Count married a rich heiress, a lass of fifteen, who was a Jewess by birth
5. The Duke called the hunter to his presence and asked him how he had caught the tiger.
6. The ways of the tempter, the enchanter, the wizard, and the sorcerer are the same.

7. The prince declared that the author had been his sole benefactor.
8. The abbot declared that the waiter was a traitor and murderer.
9. The Mayor was the patron of art and learning.
10. This shepherd once acted as a host to the Marquis.
11. His uncle is a widower and his brother is a bachelor.
12. The landlady accompanied by her maidservants went to the temple to pray to goddess for her husband's speedy return.
13. The conductor led the king and his wife to the emperor.
14. When the queen saw her father she alighted from her horse and knelt before him.
15. The monk played the part of the hero.

Ans. ....

❑❑❑

WORKSHEET-32

Name	Class..............	Roll No..........	Time 35 Min.	Max. Marks 30	Marks Obtained

I. Give the feminine of the following: **(10)**

1. Man	**6.** He-bear	**11.** Tailor	**16.** Peacock
2. King	**7.** Son	**12.** Master	**17.** Grandfather
3. Husband	**8.** Mr.	**13.** Tiger	**18.** Host
4. Drake	**9.** Lion	**14.** Hero	**19.** Cock-sparrow
5. Cock	**10.** God	**15.** Milkman	**20.** Landlord

Ans. **1.** .... **11.** ....

2. .... **12.** ....

3. .... **13.** ....

4. .... **14.** ....

5. .... **15.** ....

6. .... **16.** ....

7. .... **17.** ....

8. .... **18.** ....

9. .... **19.** ....

10. .... **20.** ....

II. Rewrite the following sentences by changing the gender: **(1 × 10 = 10)**

1. She is the heiress to this big estate.
2. When are you expecting your uncle?
3. The bridegroom was a lad of fourteen.
4. The headmaster gave away the prizes.
5. The widower is the father of four sons.
6. He took the old gentleman for a widower.
7. A hunter killed a tiger, a stag and a lion.
8. The tailor asked the priest to feed his horse.
9. A hunter requested a shepherd to tell him when the tigress was last seen.
10. The bitch came bounding to meet its master.

Ans. ....

....

....

....

....

....

....

....

....

....

....

....

....

III. Give the masculine of the following: **(½ × 20 = 10)**

1.	Bride	**6.**	Witch	**11.**	Poetess	**16.**	Lass
2.	Actress	**7.**	Niece	**12.**	Ewe	**17.**	Cow
3.	Madam	**8.**	Nun	**13.**	Hind	**18.**	Duck
4.	empress	**9.**	Bitch	**14.**	Mare	**19.**	Mother
5.	Aunt	**10.**	Heroine	**15.**	Queen	**20.**	Washerwoman

Ans.

1.	**11.** ....
2.	**12.** ....
3.	**13.** ....
4.	**14.** ....
5.	**15.** ....
6.	**16.** ....
7.	**17.** ....
8.	**18.** ....
9.	**19.** ....
10.	**20.** ....

❑❑❑

GRAMMAR

WORKSHEET-33

Name	Class..............	Roll No..........	Time 25 Min.	Max. Marks 20	Marks Obtained

1. Arrange the following groups of words into a sentence: **(½ × 10 = 5)**

(a) Stone make walls do not a prison.
(b) Money you have shall.
(c) blessed the peacemakers are.
(d) just God's true and ways are.
(e) The man conscience is who happy has a clear.
(f) were few short the prayers that said we.
(g) Stepped piper the into the street.
(h) a liar I detest
(i) The up went balloon.
(j) It wonderful isn't.

Ans. ....

....

....

....

....

....

....

....

....

....

2. Identify whether the following is a sentence or not. If it is not a sentence, then correct it: (½ × 10 = 5)

(a) have I an answer.
(b) The colour of my shirt is good.
(c) toy your is red.
(d) the boy himself cut.
(e) Sheela is my sister.
(f) queen punished boy the the.
(g) Tom ran after Jerry.
(h) Indians are all we.
(i) wall dirty you made have the.
(j) Ram was a good king.

Ans. ....

....

....

....

....

....

....

....

....

....

3. **Arrange the following groups of words into a sentence:** (½ × 10 = 5)

(a) was child flying kite a the.
(b) potato a is vegetable.
(c) crying baby is the.
(d) school go students to.
(e) speak truth we should the.
(f) go by train I.
(g) farmer has goats two and cow one the.
(h) father my is doctor a.
(i) live we in India.
(j) queen brave Laxmi Bai was a.

Ans. ....

....

....

....

....

....

....

....

....

....

....

4. **Rearrange the groups of words given below to form meaningful sentences:** (½ × 10 = 5)

(a) together flock of a feather birds.
(b) me advised he law to study.
(c) pardon to him the judge prisoner the begged.
(d) a joy ever for is beauty of a thing.
(e) your watch by what time is the
(f) can tell me you the way nearest station to the
(g) Prime the minister announced relief the people to all the district of.
(h) Why to see her could not you go personally.
(i) policeman there stands the directing the traffic.
(j) have these mangoes flavour what a delicious.

Ans. ....

....

....

....

....

....

....

....

....

....

❑❑❑

WORKSHEET-34

Name	Class..............	Roll No..........	Time 15 Min.	Max. Marks 8	Marks Obtained

1. In the following paragraph, one word has been omitted from each line. Write the missing word along with the word that comes before and the word that comes after it, in your answer sheet Do not forget to underline the word that you have supplied. The first one has been done as an example. **(½ × 8 = 4)**

		Before	**Word**	**After**
Walking very beneficial to us.	e.g.	Walking	is	very
We should get up early the morning	**(a)**	....	....	....
and go for a walk. Those are	**(b)**	....	....	....
used to for morning walks, will find it	**(c)**	....	....	....
impossible to remain bed in the	**(d)**	....	....	....
morning. For them it not much	**(e)**	....	....	....
an exercise but pleasure. It been	**(f)**	....	....	....
observed that more more Indians are	**(g)**	....	....	....
becoming health conscious and be seen	**(h)**	....	....	....
on the roads in the morning.				

Ans.

	Before	**Word**	**After**
a.	....	....	....
b.	....	....	....
c.	....	....	....
d.	....	....	....
e.	....	....	....
f.	....	....	....
g.	....	....	....
h.	....	....	....

2. In the passage given below, one word has been omitted in each line. Write the missing word along with the word that comes before and the word that comes after it in your answer sheet. Ensure that the word that forms your answer is underlined. The first one has been done as an example. **(½ × 8 = 4)**

		Before	**Word**	**After**
Dr. Loop, the father modern bypass	e.g.	father	of	modern
surgery was not only expert surgeon,	**(a)**	....	....	....
but an administrator par excellence.	**(b)**	....	....	....
It is rare find someone who combines	**(c)**	....	....	....
the two as well Dr. Loop did. He	**(d)**	....	....	....
practised cardiothoracic surgery thirty	**(e)**	....	....	....
years headed the Department of Surgery at	**(f)**	....	....	....
the Cleveland Clinic 1975 to 1989	**(g)**	....	....	....
and turned around fortunes of this	**(h)**	....	....	....
hospital.				

Ans.	Before	Word	After
a.	....	....	....
b.	....	....	....
c.	....	....	....
d.	....	....	....
e.	....	....	....
f.	....	....	....
g.	....	....	....
h.	....	....	....

❑❑❑

GRAMMAR

WORKSHEET-35

Name	Class..............	Roll No..........	Time 20 Min.	Max. Marks 12	Marks Obtained

1. In the following passage one word is missing in each line. Supply the missing word and write it against the correct blank number along with the word before it and the one after it. (½ × 8 = 4)

		Before	**Word**	**After**
Accidents on roads be prevented	**(a)**	....	....	....
provided quality of roads is improved	**(b)**	....	....	....
and the drivers instructed in	**(c)**	....	....	....
safety rules which must follow for	**(d)**	....	....	....
their own protection. It also necessary	**(e)**	....	....	....
that the illuminations the roads	**(f)**	....	....	....
is adequate as to	**(g)**	....	....	....
prevent accidents night.	**(h)**	....	....	....

Ans.

	Before	**Word**	**After**
a.	....	....	....
b.	....	....	....
c.	....	....	....
d.	....	....	....
e.	....	....	....
f.	....	....	....
g.	....	....	....
h.	....	....	....

2. In the passage given below, one word has been omitted in each line. Write the missing word along with the word that comes before and the word that comes after it in your answer sheet against the correct blank number. The first one has been done as an example. Underline your answer. (½ × 8 = 4)

		Before	**Word**	**After**
Celebrities don't have privacy that an	e.g.	have	the	privacy
ordinary person. The most personal	**(a)**	....	....	....
details of their lives splashed on the	**(b)**	....	....	....
front pages leading dailies. Media	**(c)**	....	....	....
follows them wherever they. When	**(d)**	....	....	....
they try to things that normal people do,	**(e)**	....	....	....
like eating out or watching football game, they	**(f)**	....	....	....
run the risk of being interrupted thoughtless	**(g)**	....	....	....
autograph hounds aggressive fans.	**(h)**	....	....	....

Ans.

	Before	**Word**	**After**
a.	....	....	....
b.	....	....	....
c.	....	....	....
d.	....	....	....

e. ....

f. ....

g. ....

h. ....

3. In the following passage one word is omitted in each line. Provide the missing word along with the word that comes before and one that comes after as given in the example against each blank number. Underline the word that you have provided. (½ × 8 = 4)

Passage		Before	Word	After
A reporter interviewing a witness about	e.g.	reporter	was	interviewing
an accident. She him if he had seen	**(a)**	....	....	....
the accident taking. If he could tell	**(b)**	....	....	....
her what he seen. The witness replied	**(c)**	....	....	....
that had seen a car coming at a	**(d)**	....	....	....
very speed and hitting the scooter.	**(e)**	....	....	....
The reporter asked him the scooterist	**(f)**	....	....	....
was driving his lane. The witness	**(g)**	....	....	....
said that he was not fault	**(h)**	....	....	....

Ans. **Before** **Word** **After**

a. ....

b. ....

c. ....

d. ....

e. ....

f. ....

g. ....

h. ....

❑❑❑

WORKSHEET-36

Name	Class..............	Roll No...........	Time 20 Min.	Max. Marks 12	Marks Obtained

1. The following passage has not been edited. There is one error in each of the lines. Write the incorrect word and the correction in your answer sheet against the correct blank number. (½ × 8 = 4)

		Error	Correction
The oval office is the American Presidents formal	(a)	....	....
workspace, where he confers by the heads of states,	(b)	....	....
diplomats, his staff, and other dignitaries; which he	(c)	....	....
often addressed the American public and the world on	(d)	....	....
television or radio; and where he dealt with the issues	(e)	....	....
of the day. The first oval office was built in 1913			
in an centre of the South side of the West Wing;	(f)	....	....
on 1938 it was moved to its current location	(g)	....	....
to the south-east corner overlook the rose garden	(h)	....	....

Ans. **Error** **Correction**

a. ....

b. ....

c. ....

d. ....

e. ....

f. ....

g. ....

h. ....

2. The following passage has not been edited. There is an error in each line against which a blank is given. Write the incorrect word and the correction in your answer sheet against the correct blank number at; given in the example. Remember to underline the word that you have supplied. (½ × 8 = 4)

		Error	Correction
Deepak Parekh is wide known	e.g.	wide	widely
as a senior statesmen of Indian business.	(a)	....	....
He is respecting not just for his financial	(b)	....	....
acumen and also for his integrity and un-	(c)	....	....
flinching moral courage. He has spoke out	(d)	....	....
against corruption, misgovernance or communalism	(e)	....	....
at a time that many other leading business	(f)	....	....
persons choose to steer clear of such subjects.	(g)	....	....
Official, he handed over the Chairmanship	(h)	....	....
of HDFC to Keki Mystery in December 2013.			

Ans. **Error** **Correction**

a. ....

b. ....

c. ....

d. ....

e. ....

f. ....

g. ....

h. ....

3. The following passage has not been edited. There is an error in each line. Write the incorrect word and the correction against the correct blank number in your answer sheet. The first one has been done for you as an example: **(½ × 8 = 4)**

Passage		Error	Correction
I was work in a store that sold	e.g.	work	working
handbags and luggage while a	**(a)**	....	....
woman came in for return a	**(b)**	....	....
purse she has purchased a few	**(c)**	....	....
days early. The store policy was not	**(d)**	....	....
to take returns of use goods	**(e)**	....	....
but a woman assured that the	**(f)**	....	....
item is still brand new. Since	**(g)**	....	....
the woman was so insistent, the shopkeeper			
refunded the money and on opening the	**(h)**	....	....
purse found her keys inside the purse.			

Ans. **Error** **Correction**

a. ....

b. ....

c. ....

d. ....

e. ....

f. ....

g. ....

h. ....

❑❑❑

CHAPTER

3 GRAMMAR

WORKSHEET-37

Name	Class..............	Roll No..........	Time 20 Min.	Max. Marks 14	Marks Obtained

1. The following passage has not been edited. There is an error in each line against which a blank has been provided. Write the incorrect word and the correction in your answer sheet. **(½ × 8 = 4)**

		Error	Correction
For a last three centuries	(a)	....	....
the findings of science has had	(b)	....	....
a marked impact at society	(c)	....	....
but people on a whole have	(d)	....	....
not understood just how			
our world has being affected	(e)	....	....
nor have they cared.			
From a time of Newton	(f)	....	....
men begin to realize that	(g)	....	....
through technology, which			
was base upon the findings	(h)	....	....
of science, comforts could be gained.			

Ans. **Error** **Correction**

a. ....

b. ....

c. ....

d. ....

e. ....

f. ....

g. ....

h. ....

2. **There is an error in each line of the following passage. Write the incorrect word and the correction in the answer sheet as given in the example.** **(½ × 8 = 4)**

		Error	Correction
Electricity was supplied to a house	e.g.	was	is
through cables. In cities a	(a)	....	....
cables are usually lay underground,	(b)	....	....
but in towns or villages they	(c)	....	....
may be carried in poles.	(d)	....	....
Inside the house these	(e)	....	....
cable is connecting to a main switch.	(f)	....	....
In a emergency, the	(g)	....	....
power can be turned of from	(h)	....	....
the mains.			

Ans. **Error** **Correction**

a. ....

b. ....

c. ....

d. ....

e. ....

f. ....

g. ....

h. ....

3. **A paragraph is given below. It has four errors. Edit the paragraph, clues are given:** **(½ × 4 = 2)**

The old man came in. He <u>bow</u> to all of us. Then he removed his hat and <u>glove</u>. He handed over his things <u>for</u> the boy. The boy stood behind the old <u>mans</u> chair.

Clues :

(a) verbal mistake to be corrected.

(b) noun plural to be used.

(c) preposition to be corrected.

(d) apostrophe to be used.

Ans. a. .... c. ....

b. .... d. ....

4. **The following passage has not been edited. There is an error in each line. Write the incorrect word and the correction against the correct number in your answer sheet The first one has been done for you as an example:** **(½ × 8 = 4)**

		Error	**Correction**
Thanks to the current interest for fitness	e.g.	for	in
and health these peoples are taking.	**(a)**	....	....
In each locality we find this days	**(b)**	....	....
that some centres and clubs is springing	**(c)**	....	....
up and they are do well in their	**(d)**	....	....
venture. But fortunate they are	**(e)**	....	....
not within easy reach of more.	**(f)**	....	....
Their fee are high and the centres	**(g)**	....	....
suffer from lack in equipments.	**(h)**	....	....

Ans. **Error** **Correction**

a. ....

b. ....

c. ....

d. ....

e. ....

f. ....

g. ....

h. ....

❑❑❑

WORKSHEET-38

Name	Class..............	Roll No..........	Time 25 Min.	Max. Marks 20	Marks Obtained

I. Join these sentences using relative pronouns: **(10)**

1. Sunil Khanna has been selected to lead the Indian team. He is an old Student of our school.
2. You met a woman at the conference. She just phoned.
3. We are keen to help the villagers. Their houses have been damaged in the earthquake.
4. Mr. Madhavan has taken over as the chairman of the company. He is an eminent industrialist.
5. Some people were hurt in the accident. They were standing on the footpath.
6. I have made a statement. I stand by the statement.
7. Ananya's essay had been adjudged the best. She was quite excited about it.
8. Tea is an important export item. Tea is grown in Assam.
9. Here is a list of some spices. I want you to get them from Kerala.
10. I have said something. I am not sorry for it.

Ans. ....

....

....

II. Fill in the blanks with suitable indefinite pronouns: **(½ × 10 = 5)**

1. I pressed the call bell several times but .... answered.
2. You look tired and hungry. Would you have .... to eat?
3. If there is .... you want, please let me know.
4. .... saw him entering the minister's house.
5. These facts are known to .... There is nothing secret at all.
6. I don't think .... has the courage to act against her wishes.
7. Could .... of you accompany me to the market?
8. .... could have answered these questions. They are so easy.
9. .... wanted to say .... openly.
10. All the doors were closed. So I heard absolutely ....

Ans. 1. .... 6. ....

2. .... 7. ....

3. .... 8. ....

4. .... 9. ....

5. .... 10. ....

III. Fill in the blanks with suitable reflexive or emphasising pronouns: **(½ × 10 = 5)**

1. Children, I am sure you enjoyed .... at the party.
2. The plan .... was fine but you did not explain it properly.
3. You are holding a sharp knife. Be careful lest you should cut..................
4. We have often made the same mistake ....
5. She is looking very pleased with .... Anything special?
6. He slipped in the bathroom and hurt ....
7. The buffalo defended .... bravely when a lion attacked it.
8. He amused .... by playing with the dog.
9. We should blame .... instead of holding others responsible.
10. You .... wanted to change your school, why are you complaining now?

Ans. 1. .... 6. ....

2. .... 7. ....

3. .... 8. ....

4. .... 9. ....

5. .... 10. ....

❑❑❑

Name	Class.............	Roll No..........	Time 20 Min.	Max. Marks 16	Marks Obtained

1. Fill in the blanks with suitable words by choosing the most appropriate options from the ones given below: **(½ × 8 = 4)**

That morning I awoke (a) .... the sound of steady drizzle which sounded (b) .... tiny hoof-beats upon the roof. Out of the window the prospect (c) .... quite grey and drab. And the truth was apparent (d) .... me—the outing that my friend and I (e) .... planned for this holiday would definitely be cancelled. There would be no question of that excursion (f) .... place. I was decidedly (g) .... as I had placed great store upon that excursion taking place. But I had to console (h) .... by thinking of the proverb—Man proposes and God disposes.

(a)	(i) at	(ii) to	(iii) for	(iv) on
(b)	(i) for	(ii) just	(iii) as	(iv) like
(c)	(i) is	(ii) was	{iii) has	(iv) had
(d)	{i) at	(ii) with	(iii) to	(iv) for
(e)	(i) have	(ii) had	(iii) was	(iv) were
(f)	(i) take	(ii) taken	(iii) took	(iv) taking
(g)	(i) depressing	{ii) depressed	(iii) depression	(iv) depress
(h)	(i) me	(ii) my	{iii) I	(iv) myself

Ans. a. .... **e.** ....

b. .... **f.** ....

c. .... **g.** ....

d. .... **h.** ....

2. Complete the following passage by choosing the correct options from those given: **(½ × 8 = 4)**

I (a) .... the sack of corn meal and (b) .... it to where the canoe (c) .... and pushed the vines (d) .... branches (e) .... I took a bucket (f) .... the canoe. I filled it (g) .... water and kept it under a tree. Then I pulled out (h) .... fish lines. There were two fish which had taken the bait.

(a)	(i) take	(ii) took	(iii) takes	(iv) carries
(b)	(i) carried	(ii) carry	(iii) bring	(iv) brings
(c)	(i) was hidden	(ii) hid	{iii) hide	(iv) hiding
(d)	(i) or	(ii) but	(iii) and	(iv) of
(e)	(i) along	(ii) against	(iii) apart	(iv) along
(f)	(i) in	(ii) from	(iii) with	(iv) within
(g)	(i) from	(ii) in	(iii) into	(iv) with
(h)	(i) a	(ii) the	{iii) an	(iv) on

Ans. a. .... **e.** ....

b. .... **f.** ....

c. .... **g.** ....

d. .... **h.** ....

3. **Complete the paragraph given below by choosing the correct options from those that follow:**

(½ × 8 = 4)

According to the reports issued (a) .... the Meteorological office, there has been (b) .... fog this winter than during the (c) .... The Minister of Tourism (d) .... that the delayed flights will lead to (e) .... cancellations which in turn (f) .... mean much loss for (g) .... dependent (h) .... the tourist arrival.

(a)	(i) on	(ii) by	(iii) at	(iv) in
(b)	(i) much	(ii) more	(iii) many	(iv) most
(c)	(i) latest	(ii) latter	(iii) last	(iv) later
(d)	(i) is fearing	(ii) fears	(iii) fear	(iv) feared
(e)	(i) much	(ii) most	(iii) many	(iv) less
(f)	(i) can	(ii) must	(iii) should	(iv) will
(g)	(i) that	(ii) those	(iii) this	(iv) these
(h)	(i) in	(ii) for	(iii) upon	(iv) from

Ans. a. .... **e.** ....

b. .... **f.** ....

c. .... **g.** ....

d. .... **h.** ....

4. **Complete the following paragraph by choosing the correct words from the option given below:**

(½ × 8 = 4)

When the old lady (a) .... to her flat she saw at once that the burglars (b) .... in her absence. Though the burglars themselves (c) .... no longer there she saw at once that they (d) .... because there was a burning cigarette in the ashtray. Probably they (e) .... the lift coming up and (f) .... down the stairs. But in their hurry one of them (g) .... his wallet. The old lady called the police and all of them (h) ....

(a)	(i) return	(ii) returning	(iii) returned	(iv) had returned
(b)	(i) break	(ii) broke	(iii) had broken	(iv) were breaking
(c)	(i) be	(ii) were	(iii) was	(iv) are
(d)	(i) just leave	(ii) just leaving	(iii) are just leaving	(iv) had just left
(e)	(i) heard	(ii) hear	(iii) had heard	(iv) hearing
(f)	(i) run	(ii) were running	(iii) ran	(iv) had run
(g)	(i) had dropped	(ii) are dropping	(iii) dropping	(iv) dropped
(h)	(i) catch	(ii) were caught	(iii) had caught	(iv) are caught

Ans. a. .... **e.** ....

b. .... **f.** ....

c. .... **g.** ....

d. .... **h.** ....

❑❑❑

GRAMMAR

WORKSHEET-40

Name	Class..............	Roll No..........	Time 25 Min.	Max. Marks 20	Marks Obtained

1. **Punctuate the following passage:** **(4)**

Spring while we are writing is here the winds blow gently the birds the flowers and the buds all proclaim the coming of spring.

Ans. ....

....

....

2. **Punctuate the following sentences using full stops and commas, wherever necessary:** **(½ × 14 = 7)**

i. I do not at all blame you.
ii. I came I saw, I conquered.
iii. Madan and not you is to blame.
iv. If you have courage say it on her face.
v. A dog barking at nothing is a nuisance.
vi. Tibet the roof of the world is an old land.
vii. Health is after all the most important thing.
viii. Sir I would rather be right than be President.
ix. Friends Romans countrymen lend me your ears.
x. Then at last the eyes of Kumla were pulled out.
xi. Wealth may seek us but wisdom must be sought.
xii. The rain having stopped they left for their village.
xiii. Alexander the conqueror of the world began to weep.
xiv. Father gave me a pen a pencil an inkpot and a penknife.

Ans. ....

....

....

....

....

....

....

....

....

....

....

....

....

....

....

....

....

3. **Punctuate the following sentences using comma, semi colon and the colon:** **(½ × 10 = 5)**

i. The Gita says life is action.
ii. Man is mortal God is eternal.
iii. To err is human to forgive divine.
iv. Bacon says reading maketh a full man.
v. Pope says little knowledge is a dangerous thing.
vi. A thing of beauty is a joy for ever Its loveliness increases.
vii. Shakespeare's four great tragedies are King Lear Hamlet Othello and Macbeth.
viii. The two great books of Nehru are The Discovery of India and My Autobiography.
ix. He wants money to spend on books to read horses to ride and a palatial house to live in.
x. The rain fell in torrents the sky was dark the roads were deep in mud the way was long the weary travellers plodded on in silence.

Ans. ....

....

....

....

....

....

....

....

....

....

....

....

....

....

....

....

4. **Punctuate the following passage:** **(4)**

He said why do you come and disturb me what a nuisance you are why cant you play somewhere else can,t you see that i want to work go away at once and do not come here again.

Ans. ....

....

....

....

❑❑❑

CHAPTER

3 GRAMMAR

WORKSHEET-41

Name	Class..............	Roll No...........	Time 25 Min.	Max. Marks 20	Marks Obtained

I Rewrite the following passage using the simple present tense of the verbs given in the brackets:

(½ × 10 = 5)

All baby birds (1) .... (come) from eggs. While it is in the egg, the baby bird (2) .... (get) all the food it (3) .... (need) from the white and the golden yolk in the egg. Besides food, the baby bird (4) .... (need) warmth also. So the mother bird (5) .... (crouch) over the eggs to keep them warm. Sometimes, the father (6) .... (do) this, and sometimes the parents (7) .... (take) turns. When the baby bird is sufficiently grown up, it (8) .... (being) to squirm. Each baby bird (9) .... (have) a sharp spike on its bill. As it (10) .... (push) against the walls of the egg. The spike cracks holes in it. Soon the egg begins to split open and the little bird pushes its way out.

Ans. 1. .... **6.** ....

2. .... **7.** ....

3. .... **8.** ....

4. .... **9.** ....

5. .... **10.** ....

II. Rewrite the following passage using the correct tense. Simple present or present continuous of the verbs given in the brackets:

(½ × 10 = 5)

Sunil (1) .... (sit) in the waiting hall of his doctor's clinic. Usually he (2) .... (keep) good health. But yesterday he got drenched in rain while coming home from the school. It (3) .... (appear) that he (4) .... (now suffer) from cold, cough and a sore throat. Many people (5) .... (think) that a cold is a minor disease. So they (6) .... (not care) for it. But Sunil's experience (7) .... (tell) him that a bad cold can be very troublesome. So he (8) .... (not want) to neglect it. The doctor (9) .... (examine) some other patient. So Sunil (10) .... (wait) for his turn.

Ans. 1. .... **6.** ....

2. .... **7.** ....

3. .... **8.** ....

4. .... **9.** ....

5. .... **10.** ....

III. Rewrite the following passage using the present perfect tense of the verbs given in the brackets:

(½ × 10 = 5)

The cricket match between our school and the D.A.V. Model School is about to begin. The two teams (1) .... (already arrive) on the ground. Our team (2) .... (win) all the league matches and is placed at the top of the table. Most people think we (3) .... (get) the strongest team in the zone. Today we are playing the finals. Perhaps our coach (4) .... (tell) the captain that the pitch on this ground (5) .... (never help) the spinners. So he (6) .... (decide) to include only one spinner in the team. Saurabh, the all rounder of our team (7) .... (hurt) his leg in an accident. So he is not playing today. But Vipul, who (8) .... (take) his place in the team is also a promising player. I can see that our captain (9) .... (win) the toss and (10) .... (elect) to bat. This is going to be a tough match but I am confident of our team's victory.

Ans. 1. .... 6. ....

2. .... 7. ....

3. .... 8. ....

4. .... 9. ....

5. .... 10. ....

IV. The passage below describes a serious accident you witnessed while waiting for a bus. Rewrite the passage putting the verbs in the correct form of the past tense, either simple past or past continuous:

(½ × 10 = 5)

A serious accident (1)........ (take) place on the Mall near the Model Town bus stop at 3 p.m. yesterday. I (2)........ (wait) there for my bus. A cyclist (3)........ (go) along the left edge of the road. A DTC bus (4)........ (come) at a terrific speed from the Azadpur side. As it (5)........ (try) to overtake a Maruti van, the driver (6)........ (lose) control of the bus and it unexpectedly (7)........ (turn) left and (8)........ (hit) the Maruti van, which in turn (9)........ (knock) down the cyclist. The poor cyclist's head (10)........ (strike) against something hard and pointed and he died on the spot. The driver of the van and a number of passengers travelling in the bus were badly injured. A policeman was standing at a little distance. Some labourers were also working closeby. They all came running and took the injured to a doctor.

Ans. 1. .... 6. ....

2. .... 7. ....

3. .... 8. ....

4. .... 9. ....

5. .... 10. ....

❑❑❑

WORKSHEET-42

Name	Class...............	Roll No..........	Time 30 Min.	Max. Marks 25	Marks Obtained

I. Rewrite the following passage using the present continuous tense of the verbs given in the brackets: **(½ × 10 = 5)**

What (1) .... (is) the children in the picture (2) .... (do)? A number of eatables (3) .... (hang) from the ceiling. Four children (4) .... (try) to catch them with their mouth. They (5) .... (has) their hands behind their back. John (6) .... (eagerly look) towards a hard-boiled egg. Sarah has already plucked a bunch of grapes and she (7) .... (look greedily) at them. Lucy has not succeeded in catching anything, so she (8) .... (cry). Sam (9) .... (look) towards a piece of cheese. It is clear that the children (10) .... (have) much fun. Mother and Father are happy to see their children happy.

Ans. 1. ....
6. ....
2. ....
7. ....
3. ....
8. ....
4. ....
9. ....
5. ....
10. ....

....

II. Rewrite the following passage using the correct form of the simple present tense: **(½ × 20 = 10)**

Preet Mohan Singh (have) (1) .... a new hobby. He (like) (2) .... catching butterflies. But he (practise) (3) .... his hobby in a different way. Many naughty children (put) (4) .... the butterflies they (catch) (5) .... in closed glass jars. The butterflies (feel) (6) .... miserable in the jars. When they (flutter) (7) .... their wings (knock) (8) .... against the walls of the jars, these children (feel) (9) .... happy to see the butterflies struggling. But Preet Mohan Singh is different. He (not take) (10) .... butterflies to home. He (not put) (11) .... them in jars or bottles. Then what (he do) (12) .... ? Whenever Preet Mohan (catch) (13) .... a butterfly, he (look) (14) .... at its colours carefully. He (try) (15) .... to understand the pattern on its wings. Then he (let) (16) .... it go. After that, he (take) (17) .... out his notebook and (write) (18) .... about the butterfly he has seen. Why (he not take) (19) .... the butterflies to home? He (not do) (20) .... so because he likes them. He wants them to be free to fly wherever they want to go.

Ans. 1. ....
11. ....
2. ....
12. ....
3. ....
13. ....
4. ....
14. ....
5. ....
15. ....
6. ....
16. ....
7. ....
17. ....
8. ....
18. ....
9. ....
19. ....
10. ....
20. ....

III. Fill in the correct form of the verb. **(1 × 5 = 5)**

	Present	**Past**	**Participle**
(a)	Cut	....	....
(b)	Forget	....	....
(c)	....	Broke	....
(d)	....	......	Torn
(e)	....	Flew	....

Ans. ....

....

....

....

....

....

IV. The following passage is taken from the commentary given on the Republic Day parade. Rewrite the passage putting the verbs in the simple present or the present continuous tense : **(½ × 10 = 5)**

We (now approach) (1) .... the end of the parade. As you (know) (2) .... every year the parade (end) (3) .... with a flypast by the I.A.F. planes. Three planes, after coming very close to the saluting dais, where the President and the Chief Guest (sit) (4) .... (now shoot) (5) .... vertically upwards. The two side planes have suddenly drifted away. The one in the middle (now take) (6) .... a somersault. It has taken a full somersault and (now fly) (7) .... away. It (slowly vanish) (8) .... from sight. I (think) (9) .... it was an incredible feat. I (believe) (10) .... this year's show is certainly better than last year's.

Ans. 1. ....

2. ....

3. ....

4. ....

5. ....

6. ....

7. ....

8. ....

9. ....

10. ....

❑❑❑

GRAMMAR

WORKSHEET-43

Name	Class...............	Roll No...........	Time 20 Min.	Max. Marks 16	Marks Obtained

1. **Fill in the blanks with the correct verb forms, choosing from the alternatives given in the brackets:** **(½ × 16 = 8)**

   i. He and his brother (was / were) present in the function.
   ii. Time and tide (waits/ wait) for none.
   iii. Bread and butter (is/ are) a wholesome food.
   iv. The poet and philosopher (are/ is) dead.
   v. The orator and the statesman (has/ have) arrived.
   vi. Each day and each hour (brings/ bring) as a fresh anxiety.
   vii. Either Mohan or Sohan (are/ is) in the wrong.
   viii. Neither iron nor coal (is/ are) to be found in that country.
   ix. Neither my brother nor I (am / are) happy.
   x. Roman, as well as his friend (has/ have) won the prize.
   xi. The jury (has/ have) elected its president.
   xii. There (is/ are) a large number of girls in the class.
   xiii. The military (was/ were) called out.
   xiv. Many a man (are / is) tempted by gold.
   xv. Each of these substances (is/ are) found in India.
   xvi. Either of the two applicants (is/ are) suitable.

Ans. i. ....

ii. ....

iii. ....

iv. ....

v. ....

vi. ....

vii. ....

viii. ....

ix. ....

x. ....

xi. ....

xii. ....

xiii. ....

xiv. ....

xv. ....

xvi. ....

2. **Fill in the blanks with the correct verb forms, choosing from the alternatives given in brackets:**

(½ × 16 = 8)

i. Sachin's innings in the Titan Cup .... (was, were) one of the best in his career.
ii. Civics .... (is, are) a subject taught at school.
iii. The family .... (is, are) quarrelling among themselves over the property.
iv. Ten miles of bad road .... (lie, lies) ahead of us.
v. A friend and colleague of mine .... (is, are) retiring very soon.
vi. Neither coffee nor tea .... (is, are) good for health.
vii. Every shop and every restaurant .... (was, were) closed on Thursday.
viii. Most of the boys .... (come, comes) to the school by public transport.
ix. A lot of trees .... (was, were) felled down.
x. The workers and their leaders .... (has, have) been arrested.
xi. One of the most splendid buildings .... (has, have) been built in the Palace of Versailles.
xii. A series of dacoities .... (has, have) recently taken place in Kolkata.
xiii. None of the students present .... (was, were) happy with the decision of the Principal.
xiv. The iron and steel industry .... (has, have) been severely affected by the railway strike.
xv. Not only Sheila but also her cousins .... (is, are) doing well in sports.
xvi. The CD player as well as its speakers .... (is, are) stolen.

Ans. i. ....

ii. ....

iii. ....

iv. ....

v. ....

vi. ....

vii. ....

viii. ....

ix. ....

x. ....

xi. ....

xii. ....

xiii. ....

xiv. ....

xv. ....

xvi. ....

❑❑❑

WORKSHEET-44

Name	Class...............	Roll No..........	Time 20 Min.	Max. Marks 15	Marks Obtained

1. **In each of the following, put a verb in agreement with its subject:** (½ × 10 = 5)

   i. The Lions of the east .... an interesting book.
   ii. No news .... good news.
   iii. Mohan with his brothers and sisters .... present here.
   iv. The Chief with all his men .... killed.
   v. Every man, woman and child in the village .... wounded.
   vi. The quality of these mangoes .... not good.
   vii. A few hour's study .... enough.
   viii. Neither of the explanations .... correct.
   ix. Three parts of the business .... in my hands.
   x. He is one of the wisest and noblest kings that .... ever lived.

Ans. ....

....

....

....

....

....

....

....

....

....

....

....

....

2. **Select the correct form of the verb:** (½ × 10 = 5)

   i. He as well as you (is/are) intelligent.
   ii. Many a boy (was/were) present.
   iii. Either you or he (has/have) done it.
   iv. One of the boys (was/were) punished.
   v. Neither the children nor their mothers (was/were) admitted.
   vi. All that glitters (is/are) not gold.
   vii. Two and Two (make/makes) four.
   viii. None but the brave (deserve/deserves) the fair.
   ix. Time and tide (wait/waits) for none.
   x. Slow and steady (wins/win) the race.

Ans. ....

....

....

....

....

....

....

....

....

....

....

....

3. Correct the following sentences: **(½ × 10 = 5)**

i. The general as well as his staff were there.
ii. Plucking flowers are forbidden.
iii. Neither John nor James were present in the school yesterday.
iv. The secretary and treasurer take a walk every morning.
v. John as well as Tom are waiting for you.
vi. Mohan with his friends were caught.
vii. Every boy and every teacher have his own looks.
viii. The study of mathematics require brains.
ix. The scholar and the poet is dead.
x. Every one of the men were punished.

Ans. ....

....

....

....

....

....

....

....

....

....

....

....

....

....

❑❑❑

GRAMMAR

WORKSHEET-45

Name	Class...............	Roll No..........	Time 25 Min.	Max. Marks 20	Marks Obtained

1. Identify the Adverb and state its type: **(1 × 5 = 5)**

i. Gandhiji always spoke the truth.

ii. Kamal, you can sit down.

iii. You should eat your food slowly.

iv. I shall see you soon.

v. Never do it again.

Ans. ....

....

....

....

....

....

2. Fill in with the correct adverbs: **(½ × 10 = 5)**

i. You will begin this work ....

ii. I go for a walk .... times a week.

iii. Drive a little ....

iv. You are not feeling ....

v. She .... comes to see us.

vi. It was .... cold yesterday.

vii. Your answer has been written very ....

viii. I .... had my lunch.

ix. I get up .... in the morning.

x. Behave with your elders ....

3. Fill in the blanks with suitable Adverbs from the list given below: **(½ × 10 = 5)**

(fast, much, very, frequently, before, soon, never, here, soundly, all)

i. They visit us ....

ii. He .... tells a lie.

iii. It is a .... cold day.

iv. You are .... better now.

v. I had heard this ....

vi. Don't take long. Return ....

vii. Sita was dressed .... in green.

viii. The child was tired and slept ....

ix. The boy is weak. He cannot run ....
x. Is this a Zoo ? I do not see any animal ....

Ans. ....

4. Find out Adverbs in the following sentences and write their kinds: (½ × 10 = 5)

i. He talks decently.
ii. He often comes here.
iii. Please wake us early.
iv. The train stops there.
v. My father has gone out.
vi. You can see crows everywhere.
vii. The old man walked very slowly.
viii. We looked for her everywhere.
ix. The children ran forward.
x. Ajay spoke loudly.

Ans. ....

❑❑❑

WORKSHEET-46

Name	Class...............	Roll No..........	Time 30 Min.	Max. Marks 24	Marks Obtained

1. Choose the correct preposition given in brackets: **(½ × 10 = 5)**

i. Is she related (with/ to) you?
ii. They walked (in/ into) the room.
iii. He aimed his gun (at/ on) the robber.
iv. The cat is sitting (in/under)the table.
v. He killed the snake (by/ with) a stick.
vi. He agrees (with/ to) me on this point.
vii. She came and sat (besides/ beside) me.
viii. I shall be waiting (for/ with) you here.
ix. We were in the hospital (to/ till) 4'O clock.
x. Sachin is popular (between/ among) the cricketers.

Ans. ....

....

....

....

....

....

....

....

....

....

....

2. Choose the correct preposition and fill in each blank: **(½ × 10 = 5)**

i. The cat fell .... the well. (into, in)
ii. The player was accused .... receiving bribe. (for, of)
iii. He wrote the letter .... a fountain pen. (by, with)
iv. I have been ill .... ten days. (since, for)
v. I met him .... the way. (on, in)
vi. The dacoits set the house .... fire, (on, to)
vii. I cannot agree .... your proposal of marriage. (with, to)
viii. I went to his house and remained there .... 3 O'clock. (upto, till)
ix. Place the lamp .... the table. (on, upon)
x. I am entitled .... three months' salary. (for, to)

3. **Fill in the blanks with appropriate prepositions:** **(½ × 18 = 9)**

i. The enemy is .... my door.

ii. He will come .... an hour.

iii. The boy takes .... his father.

iv. The building is .... construction.

v. He fell dead .... my eyes.

vi. I was cautioned .... believing rumours.

vii. Children quarrel .... trivial matters.

viii. With the sudden death of her husband, the responsibility of the business fell .... her.

ix. The refugees have encroached .... his land.

x. Arundhati Roy was congratulated .... her receiving the Booker Prize.

xi. Nobody is exempted .... paying the Government its taxes.

xii. In a composition, do not digress .... the main idea.

xiii. I prevailed .... him to join the picnic.

xiv. He was relieved .... his responsibility.

xv. People resort .... unfair means in order to further their prospects.

xvi. He has become reconciled .... his lot.

xvii. He reconciled .... his opponent.

xviii. I am short .... funds.

4. **Fill in the blanks with suitable prepositions given below:** **(½ × 10 = 5)**

(at, on, in, for, since, to, between, among, beside, besides)

i. This is .... you and me.

ii. The sugar mill is .... the river.

iii. It has been raining .... Tuesday.

iv. Mohan Gandhi went .... a fast.

v. I met him .... the railway station.

vi. They were sitting .... the class- room.

vii. She was born .... Ranchi .... Bihar.

viii. He had been waiting for you .... an hour.

ix. .... giving me sympathy, he gave some money.

x. Pritam singh divided the property .... his three sons.

❑❑❑

CHAPTER

3 GRAMMAR

WORKSHEET-47

Name	Class..............	Roll No...........	Time 25 Min.	Max. Marks 18	Marks Obtained

1. **Supply a suitable adjective:** (½ × 10 = 5)

   i. India is a very .... country.
   ii. She is a very .... girl.
   iii. Ravi is .... than Suresh.
   iv. Sohan is the .... boy in the class.
   v. Dogs are the .... animals.
   vi. Iron is .... than any other metal.
   vii. Calcutta is one of the .... Indian cities.
   viii. This story is .... than that.
   ix. January is the .... month in the year.
   x. Birbal was a .... man.

Ans. ....

....

....

....

....

....

....

....

....

....

....

....

2. **Supply each blank with a suitable adjective in the comparative or superlative degree.** (½ × 8 = 4)

   i. Mount Everest is the .... peak in the world.
   ii. Rekha is .... than Preeti.
   iii. Rahul is the .... boy of his class.
   iv. Calcutta is the .... city of India.
   v. His father is .... than his mother.
   vi. This story book is .... than that novel.
   vii. Iron is .... than any other metal.
   viii. Ramesh is the .... of the three brothers.

3. **Pick out the adjective and say what kind of adjective each one is:** **(½ × 8 = 4)**

i. Karan is a clever boy.

ii. English is a difficult subject.

iii. Whose book did you bring?

iv. There was some water in the jug.

v. Every child was given a packet of sweets.

vi. There is enough food for every one.

vii. This fan is not working.

viii. Several buses were burnt down.

Ans. ....

....

....

....

....

....

....

....

....

....

4. **Fill in the blanks with correct degrees of comparison:** **(½ × 10 = 5)**

	Positive	Comparative	Superlative
(i)	Low	....	....
(ii)	....	Sweeter	....
(iii)	....	....	Wettest
(iv)	....	Older	....
(v)	Honest	....	....

Ans. ....

....

....

....

....

....

❑❑❑

WORKSHEET-48

Name	Class...............	Roll No...........	Time 25 Min.	Max. Marks 20	Marks Obtained

1. Insert 'a', 'an' or 'the' wherever necessary: **(4)**

Master of ass was required to take idol from shop to temple. Idol was put on back of ass and carried through main streets of city. All along way ass saw people bowing. He felt people were bowing to him and felt quite vain of himself. Finally he became so vain that he stood still and refused to leave supposed worshippers. At this master gave him severe thrashing with cane. "Oh you fool", said master, "things have not become so bad as yet that people may start worshipping asses".

Ans. ....

....

....

....

....

....

....

....

....

....

2. Fill in the blanks with 'a', 'an' or 'the', wherever necessary: **(½ × 14 = 7)**

i. Here is .... pen that you have been looking for.

ii. .... industrial fair was inaugurated in .... city.

iii. .... moon was not visible in .... sky.

iv. Would you show me .... letter you have received?

v. .... more you read, ... more you know.

vi. .... sun rises in .... east and sets in .... west.

vii. .... eggs are sold by .... dozen.

viii. .... Ganga rises in .... Himalayas and falls in .... Bay of Bengal.

ix. .... Hindustan Times has .... largest sales in .... Northern India.

x. .... Pakistan gets a lot of military help from .... U.S.A.

xi. Last evening, ... Prime Minister went to see .... President.

xii. .... fox is .... very clever animal.

xiii. I read .... interesting story in .... Bible.

xiv. .... stone hit him on .... head.

3. **Fill in the blanks with suitable articles wherever necessary:** (½ × 8 = 4)

i. .... wisdom is .... great virtue.
ii. .... wisdom of Tenali Ram is quite famous.
iii. .... Shakespeare was .... great dramatist.
iv. .... Kalidas is usually described as .... Shakespeare of .... India.
v. .... milk used to make this ice-cream is of a pure quality.
vi. .... children should drink .... milk everyday.
vii. .... mankind should love .... nature.
viii. What .... shame! You have beaten .... innocent child.

Ans. ....

....

....

....

....

....

....

....

....

4. **Insert 'a', 'an' or 'the', wherever necessary:** (½ × 10 = 5)

i. I did not enjoy dinner he gave me.
ii. They were first to reach station.
iii. Sooner it is done, better it will be.
iv. I met him year ago at home of richest man of town.
v. Black and white cow is for sale.
vi. Child was looking at pictures when there was knock at door.
vii. Last Sunday I went to school to see old teacher of mine.
viii. There is bag lying on back seat of car.
ix. She is artist married to European engineer.
x. One-eyed man cannot get driving licence.

Ans. ....

....

....

....

....

....

....

....

....

....

❑❑❑

GRAMMAR

WORKSHEET-49

Name	Class..............	Roll No...........	Time 25 Min.	Max. Marks 20	Marks Obtained

1. Fill in the blanks by using 'shall, will, should, would': **(½ × 10 = 5)**

i. He .... certainly do it.

ii. .... I send for a coolie.

iii. He .... succeed if he tries.

iv. .... he come here tomorrow?

v. He said that he .... not come.

vi. What .... we do this evening?

vii. .... that it were spring for ever!

viii. I .... teach him a lesson for life.

ix. Children .... obey their parents.

x. He .... leave for Allahabad at once.

2. Complete these sentences using *can* or *(be) able to*. Use *can* if possible; otherwise use *(be) able to*: **(½ × 10 = 5)**

i. She thinks she .... beat anybody in the class.

ii. I haven't .... revise the whole of my syllabus.

iii. .... you see the river from your housetop?

iv. I don't think I'll .... attend the wedding.

v. Ring up Alok. He may .... help you.

vi. Only your father .... help you in this situation.

vii. I am busy on Sunday, but I .... spare some time on Monday morning.

viii. Shipra is very sincere but I doubt if she .... impress her teachers.

ix. He has lots of money. He .... buy anything he likes.

x. The light is dim; but I .... read the book.

3. **Fill in the correct modal:** (½ × 10 = 5)

i. It .... rain today.

ii. He .... have finished his report.

iii. You .... not worry at all.

iv. Ravikant .... sit for hours and read books.

v. She likes chocolate and so .... he.

vi. You .... help your friends.

vii. You .... to have been stopped by your son.

viii. We .... not beg.

ix. .... God bless you with success.

x. I .... solve this question.

4. **Fill in the blanks with 'may, might':** (½ × 10 = 5)

i. .... you be happy!

ii. You .... try once again.

iii. .... I go to the fair?

iv. .... I go with you?

v. He .... be here today.

vi. She .... be at home today.

vii. .... I make a suggestion?

viii. He .... not come tomorrow?

ix. She .... come any moment.

x. He .... have been a doctor.

❑❑❑

CHAPTER

3 GRAMMAR

WORKSHEET-50

Name	Class...............	Roll No...........	Time 25 Min.	Max. Marks 20	Marks Obtained

1. Identify the conjunction: **(½ × 10 = 5)**

i. I met her while I was going to the market.
ii. He is happy though he is poor.
iii. He may do whatever he likes.
iv. The teacher told him to work hard else he will fail.
v. Be honest and kind.
vi. I waited till the train arrived.
vii. Tom runs faster than Harry.
viii. We came after they had left.
ix. I shall go whether your come or not.
x. The dog ran after the cat.

Ans. i. .... vi. ....

ii. .... vii. ....

iii. .... **viii.** ....

iv. .... ix. ....

v. .... x. ....

2. Join the following sentences with a suitable conjunction: **(½ × 10 = 5)**

i. He is a rich man. He is very humble.
ii. She did not work hard. She failed.
iii. Our car was damaged. We escaped unhurt.
iv. He was guilty. He was not punished.
v. Be quick. You will miss the train.
vi. He sells mangoes. He sells oranges.
vii. I honour him. He is a brave man.
viii. He is poor. He is honest.
ix. He sat down. He was tired.
x. Mohan works hard. Abdul works harder.

Ans. ....

....

....

....

....

....

....

....

....

....

3. Fill in the correct conjunctions: **(½ × 10 = 5)**

i. You are tired, ... you are working.
ii. She is pretty, ... her sister is ugly.
iii. I missed the class .... I was late.
iv. Work hard .... you will not pass.
v. I got a prize .... a medal.
vi. She read the story .... she liked it.
vii. Wait here .... I return.
viii. He came .... it was dark.
ix. Two .... two makes four.
x. He is hard-working .... very clever.

Ans. ....

....

....

....

....

....

....

....

....

4. Fill in the blanks choosing the correct word from the brackets: **(½ × 10 = 5)**

i. Be just .... fear not. (but, and)
ii. I mean .... I say. (that, what)
iii. I shall wait .... you return. (when, till)
iv. Either you .... he has done it. (and, or)
v. He was so tired .... he could not stand. (as, that)
vi. He will not go .... he is invited. (if, unless)
vii. I would rather die .... beg. (but, than)
viii. .... I were you, I would have not done it. (though, if)
ix. .... want of money, he gave up studies. (because, for)
x. Though he is rich .... he is a miser. (but, yet)

Ans. ....

....

....

....

....

....

....

....

....

....

❑❑❑

CHAPTER

3 GRAMMAR

WORKSHEET-51

Name	Class..............	Roll No..........	Time 25 Min.	Max. Marks 20	Marks Obtained

1. Change into Direct Speech: **(½ × 10 = 5)**

i. The captain commanded his men to stand at ease.

ii. He proposed to us that we should return home.

iii. He ordered his servant to do as he was told.

iv. The teacher advised the students to work hard and be regular in their studies.

v. The tyrant commanded them to shoot the prisoner.

vi. He requested him to wait there till he returned.

vii. He inquired of me if I knew the way.

viii. Ali asked me when I would return.

ix. He asked me whether I played football.

x. The teacher said that he was busy then.

Ans. ....

....

....

....

....

....

....

....

....

....

....

2. Change the form of the speech: **(1 × 5 = 5)**

i. The peon said, "The manager may come in the afternoon".

ii. Mother says that dinner is ready.

iii. The king will say, "The apple must be cut into two pieces".

iv. Father says that Shanti is very honest.

v. He said to me, "My brother is ill".

Ans. ....

....

....

....

....

....

....

3. **Change into Direct Speech:** **(1 × 5 = 5)**

i. The teacher said that honesty is the best policy.
ii. The mouse said that a lion had been living in the well.
iii. He said that the moon is the earth's satellite.
iv. She said that the shop stands by the roadside.
v. She said that her father helps the poor.

Ans. ....

....

....

....

....

....

4. **Change into Indirect Speech:** **(½ × 10 = 5)**

i. He said, "It may rain tomorrow".
ii. He said, "I met this man two days ago".
iii. He said, "Last night I met a fool".
iv. Afzal said, "This is the pen I like".
v. Ashok said, "Here is the stick we have been looking for".
vi. The leader said, "I will fight now or never".
vii. He said to me, "I can easily beat you in the long jump".
viii. "I have acted foolishly", said Ajay, "in what I did".
ix. The teacher said to me, "What are you doing"?
x. The rebel said to the king, "Pardon my fault sir".

Ans. ....

....

....

....

....

....

....

....

....

....

....

....

....

....

❑❑❑

GRAMMAR

WORKSHEET-52

Name	Class..............	Roll No..........	Time 20 Min.	Max. Marks 15	Marks Obtained

1. Change the voice of the sentence: **(½ × 10 = 5)**

i. He gave me a pen.
ii. Why were you beaten by them?
iii. By whom?
iv. Is a picture being drawn by you?
v. A shirt is being stitched by Vivek.
vi. I am being helped by my friends.
vii. The zebra is attacked by the lion.
viii. An ice cream is being eaten by the child.
ix. The washerman is ironing the clothes.
x. A book is being read by Kavisha.

Ans. ....

....

....

....

....

....

....

....

....

....

....

....

....

2. Change into Active Voice: **(½ × 10 = 5)**

i. A story is being read by me.
ii. I have been punished by the teacher.
iii. Roses are being plucked by her.
iv. What is being done by you?
v. By whom are you taught mathematics?
vi. Why is noise being made by you?
vii. What has been done by you?
viii. A letter was written by her.
ix. Was money wasted by you?
x. Which movie was being seen by him?

Ans. ....

....

....

....

....

....

....

....

....

....

3. Change into Passive Voice: **(½ × 10 = 5)**

i. Students are making a loud noise.
ii. Grandparents love their grandchildren a lot.
iii. Pupils respect their teachers.
iv. Lata Mangeshkar sings a sweet song.
v. The tortoise wins the race.
vi. We learn our lessons daily.
vii. Do you like chocolates?
viii. I am writing a story.
ix. The gardener is watering the plants.
x. I have bought a new bike.

Ans. ....

....

....

....

....

....

....

....

....

....

....

❑❑❑

GRAMMAR

WORKSHEET-53

Name	Class...............	Roll No..........	Time 15 Min.	Max. Marks 10	Marks Obtained

1. Change into Active Voice: **(½ × 10 = 5)**

i. Tea was being served by me.
ii. A bird was being caught by you.
iii. A book will be read by me.
iv. The stories were written by Arthur.
v. A photograph was not taken by John.
vi. Water is being drawn by women.
vii. My work had been finished by me before seven.
viii. A toy was given to him by me.
ix. An interesting story was told to me by him.
x. He is known to me.

Ans. ....

....

....

....

....

....

....

....

....

....

....

2. Change into Passive Voice: **(½ × 10 = 5)**

i. Dogs kill cats.
ii. Suraj is eating apples.
iii. He has beaten her.
iv. You helped me.
v. He sees a peacock.
vi. I do not like her.
vii. They help me.
viii. Children like toys.
ix. They enjoyed the magic show.
x. We bought clothes.

Ans. ....

....

GRAMMAR

WORKSHEET-54

Name	Class...............	Roll No...........	Time 25 Min.	Max. Marks 18	Marks Obtained

1. Fill in the blanks with suitable words: **(1 × 10 = 10)**

i. All .... Mr Khan will .... the proposal. (accept, except)

ii. Kindly .... if the .... has been signed. (check, cheque)

iii. Soon after I gave him the next .... of the medicine, he began to .... (dose, doze)

iv. The wound on her .... took a long time to .... (heel, heal)

v. I .... that a meeting is going to take place .... (here, hear)

vi. The .... of our school is a man of .... (principal, principle)

vii. Priyanka ate .... mangoes, so she is now suffering from a .... throat. (sore, sour)

viii. The thieves could not .... the jewellery because it was lying in a locked .... almirah. (steel, steal)

ix. Here is an interesting .... about a fox that lost its .... (lost, tale)

x. .... are three bedrooms in .... house. (there, their)

Ans. i. ....

ii. ....

iii. ....

iv. ....

v. ....

vi. ....

vii. ....

viii. ....

ix. ....

x. ....

2. Complete the spellings in the following words: **(1 × 8 = 8)**

i. Now draw an ang __ __ of 60 degrees.

ii. Canvas is a c __ __ rse cloth.

iii. Writing a d __ __ ry daily at night is a good habit.

iv. In this temple, there is a very old id __ __ of Lord Shiva.

v. At night, the whole place is very qui __ __ .

vi. V __ __ ns and arteries carry blood.

vii. The ship is about to sa __ __ .

viii. A serious __ __ cident took place near our house.

Ans. i. ....

ii. ....

iii. ....

iv. ....

v. ....

vi. ....

vii. ....

viii. ....

❑❑❑

THE DAY THE RIVER SPOKE

WORKSHEET-55

Name	Class............	Roll No.........	Max. Time 15 Min.	Max. Marks 11	Marks Obtained

Q. 1. What is the main theme of "The Day the River Spoke"? **[2]**

Ans. ....

....

....

....

Q. 2. How does the river in the story express its feelings? **[2]**

Ans. ....

....

....

....

Q. 3. What lessons can be learned from the interaction between the river and the people? **[2]**

Ans. ....

....

....

....

Q. 4. Who are the main characters in "The Day the River Spoke", and what roles do they play? **[2]**

Ans. ....

....

....

....

Q. 5. What story does the teacher tell in the classroom when Jahnavi enters? **[1]**

(A) A story about ships

(B) A story about King Ashoka

(C) A story about the river

(D) A story about spiders

Ans. ....

Q. 6. What is the meaning of the word "startled" as used in the story? **[1]**

(A) Speaking softly

(B) Suddenly surprised or shocked

(C) Breathing heavily

(D) Moving smoothly

Ans. ....

Q. 7. Why couldn't Jahnavi go to school before? **[1]**

(A) She didn't like school

(B) She had to look after her baby brothers

(C) She lived too far

(D) She was afraid of the river

Ans. ....

❑❑❑

CHAPTER 1

THE DAY THE RIVER SPOKE

WORKSHEET-56

Name	Class............	Roll No.........	Max. Time 15 Min.	Max. Marks 10	Marks Obtained

Q. 1. Why is Jahnavi initially not allowed to go to school? **[1]**

(A) She is too old

(B) She is a girl and needed at home.

(C) There is no school in the village.

(D) She does not want to study.

Ans. ....

Q. 2. What does the river tell Jahnavi about girls' abilities? **[1]**

(A) Girls are better than boys.

(B) Girls are just as capable as boys.

(C) Girls should not go to school.

(D) Girls should stay at home.

Ans. ....

Q. 3. How can readers relate to the story's message about nature? **[1]**

Ans. ....

....

....

Q. 4. What advice did the River give to Jahnavi? **[1]**

Ans. ....

....

....

Q. 5. What challenges does Jahnavi face in pursuing her dream of going to school? **[4]**

Ans. ....

....

....

....

....

....

....

Q. 6. What was Jahnavi's dream for the future? **[1]**

Ans. ....

....

....

....

Q. 7. Statement I: Jahnavi snuck into school while carrying little Appu.

Statement II: The teacher shouted at Jahnavi for entering the class without permission. **[1]**

(A) Only Statement I is true.

(B) Only Statement II is true.

(C) Both Statements I and II are true.

(D) Both Statements I and II are false.

Ans. ....

❑❑❑

CHAPTER

1 THE DAY THE RIVER SPOKE

WORKSHEET-57

Name	Class............	Roll No.........	Max. Time 20 Min.	Max. Marks 15	Marks Obtained

Competency-Focused Questions

Q. 1. Statement I: Jahnavi plans to become a teacher in the future.

Statement II: Jahnavi wants to help other girls in her village go to school. **[1]**

(A) Only Statement I is true.

(B) Only Statement II is true.

(C) Both Statements I and II are true.

(D) Both Statements I and II are false.

Ans. ....

Q. 2. Why do you think Jahnavi talked to the River instead of a person? **[2]**

Ans. ....

....

....

Q. 3. How did the River help Jahnavi grow as a person? **[2]**

Ans. ....

....

....

Q. 4. What role did the teacher play in Jahnavi's journey? **[2]**

Ans. ....

....

....

Q. 5. How did Jahnavi's dream reflect her character and values? **[2]**

Ans. ....

....

....

Q. 6. If you were in Jahnavi's place, would you have gone to school on your own? Why or why not? **[2]**

Ans. ....

....

....

Q. 7. **Jahnavi's journey to school was not just a walk through the fields but a journey of courage, determination and change. Describe how Jahnavi's character grows throughout the story. What lessons can we learn from her actions?** **[4]**

Ans. ....

....

....

....

....

....

....

....

....

❑❑❑

TRY AGAIN

WORKSHEET-58

Name	Class............	Roll No..........	Max. Time 20 Min.	Max. Marks 14	Marks Obtained

Q. 1. What do you think would have happened if King Bruce had not seen the spider? Would he still have tried again? Explain your thoughts. [4]

Ans. ....

....

....

....

....

....

....

Q. 2. What happens to the spider after its first climb? [1]

Ans. ....

....

....

Q. 3. How does the spider feel after falling again? [1]

Ans. ....

....

....

Q. 4. What is the main theme of the poem "Try Again"? [2]

Ans. ....

....

....

....

Q. 5. How can the message of "Try Again" be applied in everyday life? [2]

Ans. ....

....

....

....

Q. 6. How does the spider's persistence influence King Bruce's actions in the poem? **[4]**

Ans. ....

....

....

....

....

....

....

....

....

....

....

....

❑❑❑

TRY AGAIN

WORKSHEET-59

Name	Class............	Roll No.........	Max. Time 25 Min.	Max. Marks 18	Marks Obtained

Q. 1. Discuss how the poem uses the spider as a symbol to teach a lesson about resilience. **[4]**

Ans. ....

....

....

....

....

....

....

Q. 2. Describe the spider's efforts to reach its web and the challenges it faces. **[4]**

Ans. ....

....

....

....

....

....

....

Q. 3. What does King Bruce call the spider after its failures? **[1]**

Ans. ....

....

Q. 4. How close is the spider to its web in the final attempt? **[1]**

Ans. ....

....

Q. 5. How is the message of the poem "Try Again" useful in today's world? Give examples to support your answer. **[4]**

Ans. ....

....

....

....

....

....

....

Q. 6. How does the author illustrate the concept of trying again in the chapter? **[2]**

Ans. ....

....

....

....

Q. 7. What life lessons can be learned from "Try Again"? **[2]**

Ans. ....

....

....

....

❑❑❑

CHAPTER

2 TRY AGAIN

WORKSHEET-60

Name	Class............	Roll No.........	Max. Time 20 Min.	Max. Marks 15	Marks Obtained

Competency-Focused Questions

Q. 1. Assertion (A): King Bruce decided to fight again after watching the spider.

Reason (R): The spider showed persistence by trying multiple times to reach its web without giving up. **[1]**

(A) Both A and R are true, and R is the correct explanation of A.

(B) Both A and R are true, but R is not the correct explanation of A.

(C) A is true, but R is false.

(D) A is false, but R is true.

Ans. ....

Q. 2. How does the spider finally reach its web? **[1]**

Ans. ....

....

Q. 3. What does King Bruce shout when the spider succeeds? **[1]**

Ans. ....

....

Q. 4. Can you explain the role of encouragement in the chapter "Try Again"? **[2]**

Ans. ....

....

....

....

Q. 5. How can the message of "Try Again" be applied in everyday life? **[2]**

Ans. ....

....

....

....

Q. 6. Explain the moral of the poem with reference to King Bruce's experience. **[4]**

Ans. ....

....

....

....

....

....

....

....

Q. 7. How does the poet create suspense in the poem while describing the spider's attempts? [4]

Ans. ....

....

....

....

....

....

....

....

❑❑❑

CHAPTER

3 THREE DAYS TO SEE

WORKSHEET-61

Name	Class............	Roll No..........	Max. Time 20 Min.	Max. Marks 15	Marks Obtained

Q. 1. Explain the narrator's philosophy of cherishing senses. [2]

Ans. ....

....

....

....

Q. 2. The narrator emphasises the value of sight by imagining life with it for only three days. Discuss how this limited timeframe enhances the appreciation of small moments and daily beauty. [4]

Ans. ....

....

....

....

....

....

....

....

....

Q. 3. What does the narrator's experience teach us about human resilience and the ability to find joy in limitations? Provide examples from the passage to support your answer. [4]

Ans. ....

....

....

....

....

....

....

....

....

Q. 4. How can you apply the narrator's advice about using your senses to your daily routine? Give one example. **[2]**

Ans. ....

....

....

....

Q. 5. Which season is associated with trees budding, as described by the narrator? **[1]**

(A) Summer

(B) Spring

(C) Winter

(D) Autumn

Ans. ....

Q. 6. What does the narrator feel when placing their hand on a tree with a singing bird? **[1]**

(A) Sadness

(B) Fear

(C) Happiness

(D) Surprise

Ans. ....

Q. 7. What lesson does the narrator share about using senses? **[1]**

Ans. ....

....

❑❑❑

THREE DAYS TO SEE

WORKSHEET-62

Name	Class............	Roll No..........	Max. Time 20 Min.	Max. Marks 14	Marks Obtained

Q. 1. What does the narrator want to do on the third day? **[1]**

(A) Visit museums

(B) Observe people in the city

(C) Touch leaves and trees

(D) Read books

Ans. ....

Q. 2. What does the narrator urge others to do with their senses? **[1]**

(A) Take them for granted

(B) Ignore their value

(C) Use them as if they would lose them tomorrow

(D) Use only sight

Ans. ....

Q. 3. What does the narrator feel when touching a silver birch tree? **[1]**

Ans. ....

....

Q. 4. What does the narrator hope to find in spring on tree branches? **[1]**

Ans. ....

....

Q. 5. The passage ends with a powerful message: "Use your eyes as if tomorrow you would be stricken blind." What does this suggest about gratitude and living in the present? Discuss the importance of this advice in today's fast-paced world. **[4]**

Ans. ....

....

....

....

....

....

....

....

Q. 6. **How does the passage encourage readers to reconsider and value the ordinary experiences of daily life? Reflect on how this message can impact personal habits and attitudes.** **[4]**

Ans. ....

....

....

....

....

....

Q. 7. **Describe a moment when you became more aware of your surroundings. How did it affect your experience?** **[2]**

Ans. ....

....

....

....

❑❑❑

CHAPTER

3 THREE DAYS TO SEE

WORKSHEET-63

Name	Class............	Roll No..........	Max. Time 20 Min.	Max. Marks 16	Marks Obtained

Competency-Focused Questions

Q. 1. What is the narrator's advice for appreciating music? **[1]**

(A) Listen as if you were deaf tomorrow

(B) Play musical instruments

(C) Compose songs

(D) Attend orchestras regularly

Ans. ....

Q. 2. Two statements are given - Assertion (A) and Reason (R). Read them carefully and choose the correct option. **[1]**

Assertion (A): The narrator considers sight the most delightful of all senses.

Reason (R): The narrator finds immense pleasure in touch but believes sight reveals greater beauty.

Codes:

(A) Both (A) and (R) are true, and (R) is the correct explanation of (A).

(B) Both (A) and (R) are true, but (R) is not the correct explanation of (A).

(C) (A) is true, but (R) is false.

(D) (A) is false, but (R) is true.

Ans. ....

Q. 3. If you had to give up one sense for a day, which one would you choose and why? **[2]**

Ans. ....

....

....

Q. 4. How can being mindful of the senses improve relationships with others? Give a practical example. **[2]**

Ans. ....

....

....

Q. 5. The narrator finds beauty in simple things like the bark of a tree. Mention one such simple thing in your life that brings you joy and explain why. **[2]**

Ans. ....

....

....

Q. 6. What does the narrator's experience teach us about human resilience and the ability to find joy in limitations? Provide examples from the passage to support your answer. [4]

Ans. ....

....

....

....

....

....

....

....

Q. 7. Describe how the author uses vivid language and sensory details to create strong mental imagery for the reader. How does this technique help readers understand the narrator's perspective? [4]

Ans. ....

....

....

....

....

....

....

....

....

❑❑❑

CHAPTER 4

ANIMALS, BIRDS AND DR. DOLITTLE

WORKSHEET-64

Name	Class............	Roll No.........	Max. Time 15 Min.	Max. Marks 11	Marks Obtained

Q. 1. What is the main theme of "Animals, Birds, and Dr. Dolittle"? **[2]**

Ans. ....

....

....

Q. 2. How does Dr. Dolittle communicate with animals? **[2]**

Ans. ....

....

....

Q. 3. What lessons can be learned from Dr. Dolittle's interaction with the plough horse? **[2]**

Ans. ....

....

....

Q. 4. Who are the main characters in the story, and what roles do they play? **[2]**

Ans. ....

....

....

Q. 5. Why did Dr. Dolittle stop treating humans? **[1]**

(A) He disliked humans

(B) Polynesia convinced him animals needed care

(C) He wanted to travel

(D) He lost his medical license

Ans. ....

....

....

Q. 6. What does the word "spectacles" mean in the story? **[1]**

(A) Magic tools **(B)** Eye protection glasses

(C) Decorative jewelry **(D)** Scientific instruments

Ans. ....

Q. 7. What was the plough horse's main problem? **[1]**

(A) Broken leg

(B) Blindness in one eye

(C) Stomach ache

(D) Fear of noise

Ans. ....

❑❑❑

CHAPTER

4 ANIMALS, BIRDS AND DR. DOLITTLE

WORKSHEET-65

Name	Class............	Roll No.........	Max. Time 15 Min.	Max. Marks 10	Marks Obtained

Q. 1. What motivated Dr. Dolittle to treat animals? **[1]**

(A) Fame

(B) Polynesia's advice and animal suffering

(C) Money

(D) Boredom

Ans. ....

Q. 2. What did Polynesia teach Dr. Dolittle? **[1]**

(A) Magic spells

(B) Animal languages and communication

(C) Human medicine

(D) Farming techniques

Ans. ....

Q. 3. How can readers relate to the story's message about empathy? **[1]**

Ans. ....

....

Q. 4. What advice did Polynesia give to Dr. Dolittle? **[1]**

Ans. ....

....

Q. 5. Describe the challenges Dr. Dolittle faced after becoming an animal doctor. **[4]**

Ans. ....

....

....

....

....

....

....

....

....

Q. 6. What was Dr. Dolittle's ultimate goal? **[1]**

Ans. ....

....

Q. 7. Statement I: Dr. Dolittle installed labelled doors for animals. **[1]**

Statement II: The plough horse refused to wear spectacles.

(A) Both are true

(B) Only I is true

(C) Only II is true

(D) Both are false

Ans. ....

❑❑❑

ANIMALS, BIRDS AND DR. DOLITTLE

WORKSHEET-66

Name	Class............	Roll No.........	Max. Time 15 Min.	Max. Marks 10	Marks Obtained

Competency-Focused Questions

Q. 1. Statement I: Dr. Dolittle wanted to cure all animals. **[1]**

Statement II: Dr. Dolittle aimed to become famous.

(A) Only I is true

(B) Only II is true

(C) Both are true

(D) Both are false

Ans. ....

Q. 2. Why did Dr. Dolittle trust Polynesia? **[1]**

Ans. ....

....

....

Q. 3. How did Polynesia help Dr. Dolittle grow? **[1]**

Ans. ....

....

....

Q. 4. What role did the plough horse play in the story? **[1]**

Ans. ....

....

....

Q. 5. How did Dr. Dolittle's actions reflect his values? **[1]**

Ans. ....

....

....

Q. 6. If you were Dr. Dolittle, would you have switched to treating animals? Why? **[1]**

Ans. ....

....

....

Q. 7. Describe Dr. Dolittle's character growth. What lessons does his journey teach? **[4]**

Ans. ....

....

....

....

....

....

....

....

....

....

❑❑❑

CHAPTER

5 A FUNNY MAN

WORKSHEET-67

Name	Class............	Roll No..........	Max. Time 15 Min.	Max. Marks 7	Marks Obtained

Q. 1. What is the main theme of the poem "Funny Man"? **[1]**

(A) Sadness and loss

(B) Humour and absurdity

(C) Adventure and bravery

(D) Friendship and loyalty

Ans. ....

Q. 2. Which line from the poem uses alliteration? **[1]**

(A) "He wore a shoe upon his head"

(B) "Such a funny feeling sound"

(C) "He held it to my nose"

(D) "And hopped home on his head"

Ans. ....

Q. 3. What does the word "absurd" mean in the poem? **[1]**

(A) Logical

(B) Ridiculously silly

(C) Serious

(D) Beautiful

Ans. ....

Q. 4. Why does the funny man hop home on his head? **[1]**

(A) To show off his strength

(B) To add humour and break logic

(C) To reach home faster

(D) To scare the poet

Ans. ....

Q. 5. What is the rhyme scheme of the poem? **[1]**

(A) ABAB

(B) AABB

(C) ABCB

(D) Free verse

Ans. ....

Q. 6. Describe the funny man's character traits. How do they create humour? **[2]**

Ans. ....

....

....

....

....

....

....

....

....

....

❑❑❑

CHAPTER

5 A FUNNY MAN

WORKSHEET-68

Name	Class............	Roll No.........	Max. Time 10 Min.	Max. Marks 6	Marks Obtained

Q. 1. Write a short humorous poem inspired by "Funny Man." **[2]**

Example:

There was a man from the town,

Who wore his pajamas upside-down.

Ans. ....

....

....

....

....

....

....

....

....

....

....

....

Q. 2. Compare the funny man's actions to a modern-day clown or street performer. **[2]**

Ans. ....

....

....

....

....

....

....

....

....

....

Q. 3. What lesson does the poem teach about creativity and individuality? **[2]**

Ans. ....

....

....

....

....

....

....

....

....

....

❑❑❑

A FUNNY MAN

WORKSHEET-69

Name	Class............	Roll No.........	Max. Time 15 Min.	Max. Marks 10	Marks Obtained

Competency-Focused Questions

Q. 1. Statement I: The Funny Man's actions were completely nonsensical. [1]

Statement II: The Funny Man's behaviour had a deeper meaning.

(A) Only I is true

(B) Only II is true

(C) Both are true

(D) Both are false

Ans. ....

Q. 2. Why did the poet find the Funny Man amusing? [1]

Ans. ....

....

....

Q. 3. How did the Funny Man's unusual behaviour challenge normal expectations? [1]

Ans. ....

....

....

Q. 4. What role did the Funny Man's actions play in shaping the tone of the poem? [1]

Ans. ....

....

....

Q. 5. How did the Funny Man's interactions with the poet reflect his personality? [1]

Ans. ....

....

....

....

Q. 6. If you met the Funny Man, how would you react to his behaviour? Why? [1]

Ans. ....

....

....

Q. 7. **Describe the poet's perspective on the Funny Man. What lessons does the poem teach about humour and individuality?** **[4]**

Ans. ....

....

....

....

....

....

....

....

....

....

....

....

....

....

....

❑❑❑

SAY THE RIGHT THING

WORKSHEET-70

Name	Class............	Roll No.........	Max. Time 20 Min.	Max. Marks 11	Marks Obtained

Q. 1. What is the main theme of the play "Say the Right Thing"? **[2]**

Ans. ....

....

....

....

Q. 2. How does Mary's behaviour affect the guests at the tea party? **[2]**

Ans. ....

....

....

....

Q. 3. What lessons can be learned from Mary's interactions with Mrs. Harding and Mrs. Lee? **[2]**

Ans. ....

....

....

....

Q. 4. Who are the main characters in the story, and what roles do they play? **[2]**

Ans. ....

....

....

....

Q. 5. Why did Mrs. Shaw teach Mary polite phrases like "Pleased to meet you"? **[1]**

(A) To mock the guests

(B) To follow social etiquette

(C) To test Mary's memory

(D) To impress the neighbours

Ans. ....

Q. 6. What does the word "candid" mean in the story? **[1]**

(A) Rude

(B) Dishonest

(C) Frank and honest

(D) Flattering

Ans. ....

Q. 7. What was Mary's main problem during the tea party? **[1]**

(A) Forgetting names

(B) Spilling tea

(C) Being overly blunt

(D) Arriving late

Ans. ....

❑❑❑

SAY THE RIGHT THING

WORKSHEET-71

Name	Class............	Roll No.........	Max. Time 20 Min.	Max. Marks 10	Marks Obtained

Q. 1. What motivated Mary to speak her mind openly at the tea party? **[1]**

(A) Desire to embarrass her mother

(B) Innate honesty and lack of social filter

(C) Instructions from Mrs. Harding

(D) Jealousy of the guests

Ans. ....

Q. 2. What did Mrs. Shaw emphasise to Mary before the guests arrived? **[1]**

(A) Complimenting the food excessively

(B) Using polite phrases like "Pleased to meet you"

(C) Discussing politics

(D) Singing for the guests

Ans. ....

Q. 3. How can readers relate to the story's message about authenticity? **[1]**

Ans. ....

....

Q. 4. What advice did Mrs. Shaw give Mary about discussing appearances? **[1]**

Ans. ....

....

Q. 5. Describe the challenges Mary faced during the tea party. **[4]**

Ans. ....

....

....

....

....

....

....

....

....

....

Q. 6. What was the ultimate outcome of Mary's blunt remarks? **[1]**

Ans. ....

....

Q. 7. Statement I: Mary compared Mrs. Harding's hat to a "startled pigeon." **[1]**

Statement II: Mrs. Lee praised Mary's perfect manners.

(A) Both are true

(B) Only I is true

(C) Only II is true

(D) Both are false

Ans. ....

❑❑❑

SAY THE RIGHT THING

WORKSHEET-72

Name	Class............	Roll No.........	Max. Time 20 Min.	Max. Marks 10	Marks Obtained

Competency-Focused Questions

Q. 1. Statement I: Mary wanted to follow her mother's instructions perfectly.

Statement II: Mary aimed to challenge social norms with her honesty. [1]

(A) Only I is true

(B) Only II is true

(C) Both are true

(D) Both are false

Ans. ....

Q. 2. Why did Mary continue speaking her mind despite Mrs. Shaw's warnings? **[1]**

Ans. ....

....

....

Q. 3. How did Mrs. Shaw attempt to guide Mary during the tea party? **[1]**

Ans. ....

....

....

Q. 4. What significance did Mrs. Harding's hat hold in the story? **[1]**

Ans. ....

....

....

Q. 5. How did Mary's blunt remarks reflect her personal values? **[1]**

Ans. ....

....

....

Q. 6. If you were in Mary's position, would you prioritize honesty or social etiquette? Justify. **[1]**

Ans. ....

....

....

Q. 7. Describe Mary's character growth. What lessons does her journey teach about balancing honesty and social norms? [4]

Ans. ....

....

....

....

....

....

....

....

....

....

....

❑❑❑

CHAPTER

7 MY BROTHER'S GREAT INVENTION

WORKSHEET-73

Name	Class............	Roll No.........	Max. Time 20 Min.	Max. Marks 15	Marks Obtained

Q. 1. How did the burglar alarm function and why did it fail? **[2]**

Ans. ....

....

....

Q. 2. Describe the atmosphere in the house when the thief entered. **[2]**

Ans. ....

....

....

Q. 3. Narrate the events of the night when the thief entered the house. **[4]**

Ans. ....

....

....

....

....

....

....

....

Q. 4. What does the story teach us about innovation and failure? **[4]**

Ans. ....

....

....

....

....

....

....

....

Q. 5. Assertion (A): Anand thinks that Boppa disappeared into the past. **[1]**

Reason (R): Anand saw Boppa running out of the house through the back door.

(A) Both A and R are true, and R is the correct explanation of A.

(B) Both A and R are true, but R is not the correct explanation of A.

(C) A is true, but R is false.

(D) A is false, but R is true.

Ans. ....

Q. 6. What tone does Mr Sharma use when commenting on Anand's imagination? **[1]**

(A) Harsh and critical

(B) Indulgent and amused

(C) Serious and scientific

(D) Suspicious and accusing

Ans. ....

Q. 7. What theme of the story is best highlighted in this extract? **[1]**

(A) Justice and punishment

(B) Truth and honesty

(C) Curiosity and imagination

(D) Fear and courage

Ans. ....

❑❑❑

CHAPTER 7

MY BROTHER'S GREAT INVENTION

WORKSHEET-74

Name	Class............	Roll No.........	Max. Time 15 Min.	Max. Marks 9	Marks Obtained

Q. 1. Assertion (A): Papa was angry after opening the front door. **[1]**

Reason (R): He got drenched because Anand's burglar alarm poured water on him.

(A) Both A and R are true, and R is the correct explanation of A.

(B) Both A and R are true, but R is not the correct explanation of A.

(C) A is true, but R is false.

(D) A is false, but R is true.

Q. 2. Match the words with their meanings: **[1]**

	Column A		Column B
1.	Scowling	A.	Extremely wet
2.	Sopping	B.	Rough or violent looking
3.	Ruffianly	C.	Angry facial expression
4.	Groggily	D.	In a sleepy manner

Ans. ....

Q. 3. What makes Anand believe that his time machine was successful? **[2]**

Ans. ....

....

....

....

Q. 4. What inspired Anand to create a time machine? **[1]**

Ans. ....

....

Q. 5. What makes Anand's character both funny and admirable? **[2]**

Ans. ....

....

....

....

Q. 6. Why did the children not inform the police about the missing thief? **[1]**

Ans. ....

....

Q. 7. Which of these is *false* about the thief, Boppa? **[1]**

(A) He was a regular house helper.

(B) He knew when houses were empty.

(C) He escaped through the backdoor.

(D) He was never seen again.

Ans. ....

❑❑❑

CHAPTER

7 MY BROTHER'S GREAT INVENTION

WORKSHEET-75

Name	Class............	Roll No..........	Max. Time 20 Min.	Max. Marks 14	Marks Obtained

Competency-Focused Questions

Q. 1. Assertion (A): Anita was annoyed with Anand's experiments. **[1]**

Reason (R): She was jealous of Anand's talent and popularity.

(A) Both A and R are true, and R is the correct explanation of A.

(B) Both A and R are true, but R is not the correct explanation of A.

(C) A is true, but R is false.

(D) A is false, but R is true.

Ans. ....

Q. 2. Which of the following is *true* about Anita? **[1]**

(A) She supported Anand blindly in all his inventions.

(B) She was cautious but still helped Anand.

(C) She disliked Anand completely.

(D) She reported Anand's mischief to their parents.

Ans. ....

Q. 3. How did Anita contribute to managing the crisis at night? **[2]**

Ans. ....

....

....

....

Q. 4. Why is the ending of the story left ambiguous? **[2]**

Ans. ....

....

....

....

Q. 5. What item did the children find near the time machine that belonged to Boppa? **[2]**

Ans. ....

....

....

....

Q. 6. **Do you think the children truly believed the thief time-travelled? Why or why not?** **[2]**

Ans. ....

....

....

....

Q. 7. **Discuss how the title "Dreams and Discoveries" fits the theme of the story.** **[4]**

Ans. ....

....

....

....

....

....

....

....

....

❑❑❑

PAPER BOATS

WORKSHEET-76

Name	Class............	Roll No.........	Max. Time 20 Min.	Max. Marks 15	Marks Obtained

Q. 1. How does "Paper Boats" reflect the innocence and creativity of childhood? **[4]**

Ans. ....

....

....

....

....

....

....

Q. 2. Explain how the poet's use of imagery strengthens the themes of the poem. **[4]**

Ans. ....

....

....

....

....

....

....

Q. 3. How does the poet combine imagination and real-life actions in the poem? **[2]**

Ans. ....

....

....

....

Q. 4. What do the fairies represent in the poet's dream? **[2]**

Ans. ....

....

....

....

Q. 5. **What does the act of floating paper boats reveal about the poet's personality?** **[1]**

Ans. ....

....

Q. 6. **Why does the poet use shiuli flowers in his boats?** **[1]**

Ans. ....

....

Q. 7. **How does the poet relate the clouds to his paper boats?** **[1]**

Ans. ....

....

❑❑❑

PAPER BOATS

WORKSHEET-77

Name	Class............	Roll No..........	Max. Time 20 Min.	Max. Marks 16	Marks Obtained

Q. 1. **What does the poet dream about at night?** **[1]**

Ans. ....

....

Q. 2. **How does the poet show his connection to nature in the poem?** **[1]**

Ans. ....

....

Q. 3. **How does the poet express his longing for friendship or connection?** **[2]**

Ans. ....

....

....

Q. 4. **Why is the use of nature important in the poem?** **[2]**

Ans. ....

....

....

Q. 5. **What role does hope play in the poem "Paper Boats"?** **[4]**

Ans. ....

....

....

....

....

....

....

....

....

....

Q. 6. What moral or emotional value can be learned from the poem? **[2]**

Ans. ....

....

....

Q. 7. How does the poem connect the child's inner world with the larger universe? **[4]**

Ans. ....

....

....

....

....

....

....

....

❑❑❑

CHAPTER

8 PAPER BOATS

WORKSHEET-78

Name	Class............	Roll No.........	Max. Time 25 Min.	Max. Marks 20	Marks Obtained

Competency-Focused Questions

Q. 1. What does the poet imagine about the person who might find his boat? **[1]**

Ans. ....

....

Q. 2. What do the "paper boats" symbolise in the poem? **[2]**

Ans. ....

....

....

....

Q. 3. What does the act of launching paper boats daily suggest about the child? **[2]**

Ans. ....

....

....

....

Q. 4. How do the poet's daydreams differ from his night-time dreams? **[2]**

Ans. ....

....

....

....

Q. 5. Discuss how Rabindranath Tagore uses contrast between day and night in the poem. **[4]**

Ans. ....

....

....

....

....

....

....

Q. 6. How is the poem "Paper Boats" an expression of universal childhood? **[4]**

Ans. ....

....

....

....

....

....

....

Q. 7. How does "Paper Boats" celebrate the beauty of dreams and imagination? **[4]**

Ans. ....

....

....

....

....

....

....

Q. 8. What do the "baskets full of dreams" signify in the poem? **[1]**

Ans. ....

....

❑❑❑

CHAPTER

9 NORTH, SOUTH, EAST, WEST

WORKSHEET-79

Name	Class............	Roll No.........	Max. Time 20 Min.	Max. Marks 15	Marks Obtained

Q. 1. Describe Shaana's experience at the Thajiwas glacier in Kashmir. **[2]**

Ans. ....

....

....

Q. 2. Why did Shaana enjoy her rafting experience on the Narmada river? **[2]**

Ans. ....

....

....

Q. 3. What does Shaana's journey tell us about India's natural diversity? **[4]**

Ans. ....

....

....

....

....

....

....

....

Q. 4. How did Shaana's understanding of geography change during her travels? **[4]**

Ans. ....

....

....

....

....

....

....

....

Q. 5. Shaana compared the desert to: [1]

(A) a mountain.

(B) a beach without sea.

(C) a dry forest.

(D) a valley.

Ans. ....

Q. 6. We saw *pebbles* on the beach. [1]

(A) Seashells

(B) Round, smooth stones

(C) Tiny bugs

(D) Raindrops

Ans. ....

Q. 7. Assertion (A): Shaana found rafting in the Narmada river calm and relaxing. **[1]**

Reason (R): Rivers in India are mostly calm and slow.

(A) Both A and R are true, and R is the correct explanation of A.

(B) Both A and R are true, but R is not the correct explanation of A.

(C) A is true but R is false.

(D) A is false but R is true.

Ans. ....

❑❑❑

CHAPTER

9 NORTH, SOUTH, EAST, WEST

WORKSHEET-80

Name	Class............	Roll No..........	Max. Time 20 Min.	Max. Marks 12	Marks Obtained

Q. 1. Assertion (A): Shaana was scared of tunnels in Goa. **[1]**

Reason (R): She overcame her fear after travelling through many of them.

(A) Both A and R are true, and R is the correct explanation of A.

(B) Both A and R are true, but R is not the correct explanation of A.

(C) A is true, but R is false.

(D) A is false, but R is true.

Ans. ....

Q. 2. I crossed the *Pamban bridge.* **[1]**

(A) Bridge connecting Goa to Gujarat.

(B) Bridge across the Ganga river.

(C) Bridge connecting Rameswaram to mainland.

(D) Metro bridge in Kolkata.

Ans. ....

Q. 3. What made Shaana feel cold in the Thajiwas glacier? **[1]**

Ans. ....

....

Q. 4. What did Shaana learn during her visit to the Sundarbans? **[2]**

Ans. ....

....

....

....

Q. 5. Describe Shaana's feelings in her final letters after completing her journey. **[4]**

Ans. ....

....

....

....

....

....

Q. 6. Why did Shaana feel responsible during the surfing experience in Puducherry? [2]

Ans. ....

....

....

Q. 7. Why did Shaana call the desert a beach without the sea? [1]

Ans. ....

....

❑❑❑

NORTH, SOUTH, EAST, WEST

WORKSHEET-81

Name	Class............	Roll No.........	Max. Time 20 Min.	Max. Marks 12	Marks Obtained

Competency-Focused Questions

Q. 1. Assertion (A): Mangrove trees grow in wetlands. **[1]**

Reason (R): Wetlands have seawater that supports mangrove vegetation.

(A) Both A and R are true, and R is the correct explanation of A.

(B) Both A and R are true, but R is not the correct explanation of A.

(C) A is true, but R is false.

(D) A is false, but R is true.

Ans. ....

Q. 2. What surprised Shaana about the Sundarbans? **[1]**

Ans. ....

....

Q. 3. How did Shaana react to her visit to Goa's plateaus? **[2]**

Ans. ....

....

....

....

....

Q. 4. How did Shaana show curiosity and courage throughout her journey? **[4]**

Ans. ....

....

....

....

....

....

....

....

....

....

Q. 5. What role did Shaana's parents play in making the journey enjoyable? **[4]**

Ans. ....

....

....

....

....

....

....

....

....

....

....

....

❑❑❑

THE TUNNEL

WORKSHEET-82

Name	Class............	Roll No.........	Max. Time 20 Min.	Max. Marks 11	Marks Obtained

Q. 1. What is the main theme of "The Tunnel"? **[2]**

Ans. ....

....

....

....

Q. 2. How does Suraj feel when he first enters the tunnel? **[2]**

Ans. ....

....

....

....

Q. 3. What lesson can be learned from Suraj's adventure? **[2]**

Ans. ....

....

....

....

Q. 4. Who is Sunder Singh, and what role does he play in the story? **[2]**

Ans. ....

....

....

....

Q. 5. Why did Suraj visit the tunnel? **[1]**

(A) To find treasure

(B) To watch trains and explore

(C) To escape home

(D) To meet Sunder Singh

Ans. ....

Q. 6. What does the word "dampness" mean in the story? **[1]**

(A) Brightness

(B) Slight wetness

(C) Darkness

(D) Warmth

Ans. ....

Q. 7. What animal did Suraj think he saw after leaving the tunnel? **[1]**

(A) Tiger

(B) Leopard

(C) Wolf

(D) Bear

Ans. ....

❑❑❑

THE TUNNEL

WORKSHEET-83

Name	Class............	Roll No.........	Max. Time 20 Min.	Max. Marks 8	Marks Obtained

Q. 1. What motivated Suraj to explore the tunnel despite his fears? **[1]**

(A) Sunder Singh's warnings

(B) His curiosity and imagination

(C) A bet with friends

(D) Desire to find the leopard

Ans. ....

Q. 2. How does Sunder Singh view the jungle and its animals? **[1]**

Ans. ....

....

....

....

Q. 3. How can readers relate to Suraj's experience in the tunnel? **[1]**

Ans. ....

....

....

....

Q. 4. Describe the setting of the tunnel. How does it add to the story's mood? **[2]**

Ans. ....

....

....

....

....

Q. 5. Write a short paragraph about a time you faced a fear, like Suraj. **[2]**

Ans. ....

....

....

....

Q. 6. Statement I: The tunnel was brightly lit. **[1]**

Statement II: Suraj imagined the train as a dragon.

(A) Both are true

(B) Only I is true

(C) Only II is true

(D) Both are false

Ans. ....

❑❑❑

CHAPTER

10 THE TUNNEL

WORKSHEET-84

Name	Class............	Roll No.........	Max. Time 15 Min.	Max. Marks 9	Marks Obtained

Competency-Focused Questions

Q. 1. Statement I: Suraj's adventure was entirely safe. **[1]**

Statement II: The leopard symbolizes danger and harmony.

(A) Only I is true

(B) Only II is true

(C) Both are true

(D) Both are false

Ans. ....

Q. 2. Why does Suraj compare the train to a dragon? **[1]**

Ans. ....

....

....

....

Q. 3. How does Sunder Singh's character contrast with Suraj's? **[1]**

Ans. ....

....

....

....

Q. 4. What role does imagination play in Suraj's journey? **[1]**

Ans. ....

....

....

....

Q. 5. If you were Suraj, would you enter the tunnel again? Why? **[1]**

Ans. ....

....

....

....

Q. 6. **Describe how the story balances "danger" and "wonder." Use examples.** **[4]**

Ans. ....

....

....

....

....

....

....

....

....

....

....

....

❑❑❑

CHAPTER

11 TRAVEL

WORKSHEET-85

Name	Class............	Roll No.........	Max. Time 20 Min.	Max. Marks 11	Marks Obtained

Q. 1. What is the main theme of the poem? [2]

Ans. ....

....

....

....

....

....

Q. 2. How does the speaker feel about the trains they imagine? [2]

Ans. ....

....

....

....

....

Q. 3. What lesson does the poem convey about human desires? [2]

Ans. ....

....

....

....

....

Q. 4. What role does imagination play in the poem? [2]

Ans. ....

....

....

....

....

....

Q. 5. Why does the speaker mention "voices speaking" during the day? **[1]**

(A) To show the noise of reality

(B) To describe a crowded station

(C) To highlight friends talking

(D) To criticise loud people

Ans. ....

Q. 6. What does "cinders red on the sky" symbolise? **[1]**

(A) Pollution from trains

(B) The speaker's vivid imagination

(C) A sunset

(D) Fireworks

Ans. ....

Q. 7. Which word means "a loud, sharp cry"? **[1]**

(A) Steaming

(B) Shrieking

(C) Still

(D) Knowing

Ans. ....

❑❑❑

CHAPTER 11

TRAVEL

WORKSHEET-86

Name	Class............	Roll No.........	Max. Time 15 Min.	Max. Marks 8	Marks Obtained

Q. 1. What motivates the speaker to imagine trains? [1]

(A) Fear of silence

(B) Desire for adventure

(C) Love for locomotives

(D) Hatred for friends

Ans. ....

Q. 2. How does the poem contrast day and night? [1]

Ans. ....

....

....

....

....

Q. 3. How does the line "My heart is warm with the friends I make" conflict with the speaker's desires? [1]

Ans. ....

....

....

....

....

Q. 4. Identify a literary device in "hear its whistle shrieking" and explain its effect. [2]

Ans. ....

....

....

....

....

....

....

....

Q. 5. **Write a stanza (4 lines) about longing for something you can't have, inspired by the poem.** **[2]**

Ans. ....

....

....

....

....

....

....

Q. 6. **Statement I: The speaker hears real trains.** **[1]**

Statement II: The poem uses imagery of fire and sound.

(A) Both are true

(B) Only I is true

(C) Only II is true

(D) Both are false

Ans. ....

❑❑❑

Name	Class............	Roll No.........	Max. Time 15 Min.	Max. Marks 9	Marks Obtained

Competency-Focused Questions

Q. 1. Statement I: The trains symbolise freedom. [1]

Statement II: The speaker hates their current life.

(A) Only I is true

(B) Only II is true

(C) Both are true

(D) Both are false

Ans. ....

Q. 2. Why does the speaker say "there isn't a train I wouldn't take"? [1]

Ans. ....

....

....

....

Q. 3. How does the poem use sound to reflect the speaker's emotions? [1]

Ans. ....

....

....

....

Q. 4. What does the phrase "better friends I'll not be knowing" reveal? [1]

Ans. ....

....

....

....

Q. 5. If you were the speaker, would you board the train? Why? [1]

Ans. ....

....

....

....

Q. 6. Analyse how the poem blends reality and imagination. Use examples. **[4]**

Ans. ....

....

....

....

....

....

....

....

....

....

....

....

....

....

❑❑❑

CHAPTER 12

CONQUERING THE SUMMIT

WORKSHEET-88

Name	Class............	Roll No..........	Max. Time 20 Min.	Max. Marks 11	Marks Obtained

Q. 1. **What is the main theme of "Conquering the Summit"?** **[2]**

Ans. ....

....

....

....

....

Q. 2. **How did Arunima Sinha's accident change her life?** **[2]**

Ans. ....

....

....

....

....

Q. 3. **What lesson does Arunima's story teach about perseverance?** **[2]**

Ans. ....

....

....

....

....

....

Q. 4. **Who was Bachendri Pal, and why was she important to Arunima?** **[2]**

Ans. ....

....

....

....

....

....

Q. 5. Why did Arunima decide to climb Mount Everest? **[1]**

(A) To win money

(B) To prove amputees can achieve greatness

(C) To become famous

(D) To escape her family

Ans. ....

Q. 6. What does the word "resilience" mean in the chapter? **[1]**

(A) Physical strength

(B) Ability to recover from difficulties

(C) Climbing skills

(D) Financial success

Ans. ....

Q. 7. Which award did Arunima receive in 2015? **[1]**

(A) Bharat Ratna

(B) Padma Shri

(C) Arjuna Award

(D) Khel Ratna

Ans. ....

❑❑❑

CHAPTER

12 CONQUERING THE SUMMIT

WORKSHEET-89

Name	Class............	Roll No.........	Max. Time 15 Min.	Max. Marks 8	Marks Obtained

Q. 1. What motivated Arunima to keep going after her accident? **[1]**

(A) Financial rewards

(B) Her desire to inspire others

(C) Family pressure

(D) Fear of failure

Ans. ....

Q. 2. How did Bachendri Pal's guidance impact Arunima's journey? **[1]**

Ans. ....

....

....

Q. 3. Why did Arunima leave Swami Vivekananda's photo on Everest? **[1]**

Ans. ....

....

....

Q. 4. Identify a key challenge Arunima faced during her training. **[2]**

Ans. ....

....

....

....

....

Q. 5. Write a short paragraph about a time you overcame a fear, inspired by Arunima. **[2]**

Ans. ....

....

....

....

....

Q. 6. Statement I: Arunima climbed only Mount Everest. **[1]**

Statement II: She became the first female amputee to complete the Seven Summits.

(A) Both are true

(B) Only I is true

(C) Only II is true

(D) Both are false

Ans. ....

❑❑❑

CHAPTER

12 CONQUERING THE SUMMIT

WORKSHEET-90

Name	Class............	Roll No..........	Max. Time 15 Min.	Max. Marks 9	Marks Obtained

Competency-Focused Questions

Q. 1. Statement I: Arunima's accident was a setback with no positive outcomes. **[1]**

Statement II: Her story emphasises that goals require sacrifice.

(A) Only I is true

(B) Only II is true

(C) Both are true

(D) Both are false

Ans. ....

Q. 2. Why is Arunima called a "beacon of hope"? **[1]**

Ans. ....

....

Q. 3. How does the chapter highlight the importance of mentorship? **[1]**

Ans. ....

....

Q. 4. What does planting the Indian flag on Everest symbolise? **[1]**

Ans. ....

....

Q. 5. If you were Arunima, what would you do after climbing Everest? **[1]**

Ans. ....

....

Q. 6. Analyse how Arunima's journey reflects the quote: "The only disability in life is a bad attitude." **[4]**

Ans. ....

....

....

....

....

❑❑❑

CHAPTER

13 A HOMAGE TO OUR BRAVE SOLDIERS

WORKSHEET-91

Name	Class............	Roll No.........	Max. Time 20 Min.	Max. Marks 11	Marks Obtained

Q. 1. What impression did the visit to the National War Memorial leave on the narrator? [2]

Ans. ....

....

....

....

Q. 2. Why is the National War Memorial more than just a structure? [2]

Ans. ....

....

....

....

Q. 3. What features make the National War Memorial unique and meaningful? [2]

Ans. ....

....

....

....

Q. 4. Explain how the National War Memorial represents courage and sacrifice. [2]

Ans. ....

....

....

....

Q. 5. What does the eternal flame at the memorial represent? [1]

Ans. ....

....

Q. 6. Why are wreaths placed at the obelisk in the National War Memorial? [1]

Ans. ....

....

Q. 7. How does the lighting design of the memorial change throughout the day? **[1]**

Ans. ....

....

❑❑❑

CHAPTER

13 A HOMAGE TO OUR BRAVE SOLDIERS

WORKSHEET-92

Name	Class............	Roll No.........	Max. Time 20 Min.	Max. Marks 10	Marks Obtained

Q. 1. What makes the National War Memorial a symbol of patriotism? **[1]**

Ans. ....

....

Q. 2. Why did the narrator feel overwhelmed at the memorial? **[1]**

Ans. ....

....

Q. 3. What impression does the lighting design leave on visitors? **[1]**

Ans. ....

....

Q. 4. How do war memorials instil patriotism in young citizens? **[1]**

Ans. ....

....

Q. 5. Describe the emotional impact of visiting the National War Memorial. **[4]**

Ans. ....

....

....

....

....

....

....

....

....

....

....

....

....

Q. 6. How does the lighting at the memorial enhance its beauty? **[1]**

Ans. ....

....

Q. 7. What does Ananda mean when she calls it a 'supreme' sacrifice? **[1]**

Ans. ....

....

❑❑❑

CHAPTER

13 A HOMAGE TO OUR BRAVE SOLDIERS

WORKSHEET-93

Name	Class............	Roll No..........	Max. Time 25 Min.	Max. Marks 16	Marks Obtained

Competency-Focused Questions

Q. 1. What is the purpose of building a war memorial? [1]

Ans. ....

....

Q. 2. How does the memorial connect people emotionally to soldiers' sacrifices? [1]

Ans. ....

....

Q. 3. What message does the National War Memorial convey to citizens? [1]

Ans. ....

....

Q. 4. How does the memorial engage visitors emotionally and visually? [1]

Ans. ....

....

Q. 5. In what ways does the National War Memorial serve educational purposes for young citizens? [4]

Ans. ....

....

....

....

....

....

....

....

....

....

....

....

....

Q. 6. Why is the eternal flame a significant feature of the memorial? **[4]**

Ans. ....

....

....

....

....

....

....

....

....

....

Q. 7. What role does symbolism play in the memorial's architecture and layout? **[4]**

Ans. ....

....

....

....

....

....

....

....

....

....

....

❑❑❑

MY DEAR SOLDIERS

WORKSHEET-94

Name	Class............	Roll No.........	Max. Time 30 Min.	Max. Marks 21	Marks Obtained

Q. 1. How does the poet describe the challenges soldiers face during their service? [2]

Ans. ....
....
....
....

Q. 2. Why does the poet feel soldiers are worthy of prayers and blessings? [2]

Ans. ....
....
....
....
....

Q. 3. Describe how the poem celebrates the spirit of Indian soldiers. [4]

Ans. ....
....
....
....
....
....
....

Q. 4. What sacrifices of soldiers are highlighted in the poem? [4]

Ans. ....
....
....
....
....
....

Q. 5. **What role do soldiers play while the rest of the country sleeps?** **[1]**

Ans. ....

....

Q. 6. **What is meant by "treading the lonely expanses"?** **[1]**

Ans. ....

....

Q. 7. **Mention two natural elements that soldiers face during their service.** **[1]**

Ans. ....

....

....

❑❑❑

CHAPTER

14 MY DEAR SOLDIERS

WORKSHEET-95

Name	Class............	Roll No.........	Max. Time 20 Min.	Max. Marks 15	Marks Obtained

Q. 1. **Why does the poet compare soldiers to yogis?** **[1]**

Ans. ....

....

Q. 2. **What do the "wind chimes" symbolise in the poem?** **[1]**

Ans. ....

....

Q. 3. **Which stage of life do soldiers dedicate to the nation?** **[1]**

Ans. ....

....

Q. 4. **Explain the poetic device used in "Wind chimes of my land vibrate your feat."** **[2]**

Ans. ....

....

....

....

Q. 5. **What image of a soldier's life does the poet create in the poem?** **[2]**

Ans. ....

....

....

....

Q. 6. **In what way does the poet use nature and the landscape to show soldiers' bravery?** **[4]**

Ans. ....

....

....

....

....

....

....

Q. 7. Explain how the poem uses the comparison with yogis to deepen the respect for soldiers. [4]

Ans. ....

....

....

....

....

....

....

❑❑❑

CHAPTER

14 MY DEAR SOLDIERS

WORKSHEET-96

Name	Class............	Roll No.........	Max. Time 25 Min.	Max. Marks 19	Marks Obtained

Competency-Focused Questions

Q. 1. How does the poem express gratitude towards soldiers? [1]

Ans. ....

....

Q. 2. What does the line "still hold on to your deed" suggest about soldiers' determination? [2]

Ans. ....

....

....

....

Q. 3. What contrast does the poet present at the beginning of the poem? [2]

Ans. ....

....

....

....

Q. 4. How is the soldier's life portrayed as spiritual in the poem? [2]

Ans. ....

....

....

....

Q. 5. How does the poem create a sense of patriotism in the reader? [4]

Ans. ....

....

....

....

....

....

....

Q. 6. **What message does the poet want to convey to the readers through this poem?** **[4]**

Ans. ....

....

....

....

....

....

....

....

....

....

Q. 7. **How is the poem both a tribute and a prayer for the soldiers?** **[4]**

Ans. ....

....

....

....

....

....

....

....

....

....

❑❑❑

CHAPTER

15 RANI ABBAKKA

WORKSHEET-97

Name	Class............	Roll No.........	Max. Time 20 Min.	Max. Marks 15	Marks Obtained

Q. 1. Who was Hiriya Abbakka, and what happened to her kingdom? [2]

Ans. ....

....

....

....

Q. 2. How did the Portuguese governor react when he heard about the fall of Fort Mangalore? [2]

Ans. ....

....

....

....

Q. 3. Why did the Portuguese attack Rani Abbakka's kingdom, and how did she respond? [4]

Ans. ....

....

....

....

....

....

....

Q. 4. How did Rani Abbakka's people support her in her battle against the Portuguese? [4]

Ans. ....

....

....

....

....

....

....

Q. 5. Which Portuguese fort did Abbakka attack? **[1]**

Ans. ....

....

Q. 6. What did the Portuguese force Ullal to pay? **[1]**

Ans. ....

....

Q. 7. Who finally drove the Portuguese out of Mangalore? **[1]**

Ans. ....

....

❑❑❑

CHAPTER

15 RANI ABBAKKA

WORKSHEET-98

Name	Class............	Roll No..........	Max. Time 30 Min.	Max. Marks 21	Marks Obtained

Q. 1. **Who was the Portuguese commander that escaped after Abbakka's attack?** **[1]**

Ans. ....

....

....

....

Q. 2. **How did Rani Abbakka's refusal to pay tribute to the Portuguese impact Ullal?** **[4]**

Ans. ....

....

....

....

....

....

....

....

....

....

....

Q. 3. **What two things did Rani Abbakka refuse to provide to the Portuguese?** **[2]**

Ans. ....

....

....

....

....

....

....

....

Q. 4. **How did the soldiers react when the king ordered them to arrest Rani Abbakka?** **[2]**

Ans. ....

....

....

....

Q. 5. **What qualities made Rani Abbakka a great leader?** **[4]**

Ans. ....

....

....

....

....

....

....

Q. 6. **How did Rani Abbakka show her determination against the Portuguese?** **[4]**

Ans. ....

....

....

....

....

....

....

Q. 7. **Describe how Abbakka gathered support to fight the Portuguese.** **[4]**

Ans. ....

....

....

....

....

....

....

❑❑❑

CHAPTER

15 RANI ABBAKKA

WORKSHEET-99

Name	Class............	Roll No.........	Max. Time 25 Min.	Max. Marks 18	Marks Obtained

Competency-Focused Questions

Q. 1. What is the significance of Rani Abbakka in Indian history? **[2]**

Ans. ....

....

....

....

Q. 2. What are some key events in Rani Abbakka's life? **[2]**

Ans. ....

....

....

....

Q. 3. How did Rani Abbakka challenge Portuguese colonialism? **[2]**

Ans. ....

....

....

....

Q. 4. Why is Rani Abbakka considered a symbol of women's empowerment? **[2]**

Ans. ....

....

....

....

Q. 5. What lessons can be learnt from Rani Abbakka's leadership? **[2]**

Ans. ....

....

....

....

Q. 6. **Discuss how Rani Abbakka's story inspires others to stand up for freedom.** **[4]**

Ans. ....

....

....

....

....

....

....

....

Q. 7. **Explain the events of the battle for Ullal and its outcome.** **[4]**

Ans. ....

....

....

....

....

....

....

....

❑❑❑

WRITING YOUR NOTES

Just in case you have forgotten today, take down your notes!
But why is it so important?

Tools for the hands are tools for the brain writes Hetty Roessingh.
Handwritten notes are a powerful tool for encrypting embodied cognition and in turn supporting the brain's capacity for recuperation of information. If that sounds so scientific then in simple words: Writing notes by hand help you in:

- Increasing your comprehension
- Strengthening your memory
- Igniting your creativity
- Engaging your mind
- Increasing your attention span

Are these reasons enough to get you started?

WRITING YOUR NOTES

Just in case you have forgotten today, take down your notes!
But why is it so important?

Tools for the hands are tools for the brain writes Hetty Roessingh.
Handwritten notes are a powerful tool for encrypting embodied cognition and in turn supporting the brain's capacity for recuperation of information. If that sounds so scientific then in simple words: Writing notes by hand help you in:

- ◆ Increasing your comprehension ◆ Strengthening your memory ◆ Igniting your creativity
- ◆ Engaging your mind ◆ Increasing your attention span

Are these reasons enough to get you started?